Praise for

Excellent read...True t̶o̶ ̶A̶l̶a̶s̶k̶a̶.̶ ̶B̶e̶n̶ ̶H̶u̶n̶n̶i̶c̶u̶t̶t̶ ̶u̶s̶e̶s̶ ̶s̶k̶i̶l̶l̶, luck, and intuition to solve a very intriguing situation. Step by step he gathers pieces of information (in the most unlikely yet realistic situations) which will lead him to an interesting finale. This book would make a wonderful movie...everyone would enjoy it, there is something for everyone from teens to seniors. This book has adventure, mystery, beautiful scenery, intrigue, partnership, surprise, and a touch of romance. I highly recommend this book to anyone wanting to read a different yet very believable and interesting story.

The hero, Ben Hunnicutt, must search Alaska for the murderer. Carefully researched, this crime procedural is richly draped in Alaska history and landscape. It's a sweet read that kept me up way past my bedtime.

From the beginning, the story got my attention and it never waned. When I finished, I knew I had to get the next book in line. Being from Alaska myself, I was familiar with the locations in this story which made it all that more interesting.

Excellent read! Alaska Cold War history, mystery, suspense. Author's first novel and first of a series. His Ben Hunnicutt series gets better and better - need to read Warhead and Crosskill also!

Excellent book! I read it with great delight and was impressed page by page and surprised by the ending. A must buy!

The Last Kill is a historically rich and realistic narrative that will leave readers ready to book a trip to Alaska.

Additional titles by Don Neal

The Ben Hunnicutt Novels

Washtub Gold
Warhead
CrossKill
The Last Kill

RED STAR DOWN

A Ben Hunnicutt Novel

Don Neal

First Edition Design Publishing
Sarasota, Florida USA

Red Star Down
Copyright ©2019 Don Neal

ISBN 978-1506-908-80-9 PBK
ISBN 978-1506-908-81-6 EBK

LCCN 2020900269

January 2020

Published and Distributed by
First Edition Design Publishing, Inc.
P.O. Box 17646, Sarasota, FL 34276-3217
www.firsteditiondesignpublishing.com

ALL RIGHTS RESERVED. No part of this book publication may be reproduced, stored in a retrieval system, or transmitted in any form or by any means — electronic, mechanical, photo-copy, recording, or any other — except brief quotation in reviews, without the prior permission of the author or publisher.

*For
Stephanie*

PROLOGUE

SOMEWHERE OVER ALASKA

MARCH, 1944

CIRCLES

The Douglas C-47 Skytrain traced tight circles in the northern sky, as tight as could be maintained without losing precious altitude. The pilot, one Lieutenant Dmitry Pavlovich, stared through the gray murk beyond. He sincerely hoped that his circles were well above any stony mountain peak that might threaten to rip the guts out of his airplane; if fate decreed otherwise, there was still the slim hope that he might see the threat in time to avoid it.

The navigator, Viktor Popov, hunched beside his pilot, navigation charts across his knees, straining his eyes for any landmark which might help locate the aircraft in its journey over the poorly mapped terrain of Alaska. There was little hope, he knew—the C-47 had departed the air base at Great Falls in Montana many hours before, destined for Ladd Field at Fairbanks, Alaska. It had plunged into a thick overcast while still an hour out from Fairbanks. The pilot had first climbed, then descended in an attempt to find clear weather. The changes in altitude and direction, and a compass that seemed ambivalent concerning the direction of north, combined to befuddle Popov.

With no landmark visible through the gray milk that the plane seemed to be swimming through, and with only fragmented radio contact with Ladd Field, he was completely lost.

Boris Ivanovich, the flight engineer, ignored the goings on in the flight cabin. His only concern was the continued smooth operation of the twin Pratt and Whitney radials hammering away in the wing nacelles, and with the fuel consumption of these same thirsty engines.

A tall officer standing in the doorway to the cargo bay showed obvious concern as he observed the stress on the faces of his pilot and navigator. He had a leather briefcase manacled to his left wrist, and frequently touched it with his free hand as though to reassure himself that it was still there.

The crew had no idea that a strong wind from the north was moving the entire front, their aircraft included, southward. Their circles, intended to keep them over a single, supposedly peak-free area were whirling them toward the southwest, toward a largely uncharted mountain mass east of the Gerstle River.

The officer with the briefcase stepped forward and touched the pilot on the shoulder.

"Lieutenant Pavlovich, what is our situation?"

The pilot opened his mouth to respond, but if he said anything, it went unheard.

There was a crash of sound and a shriek of tearing metal as the right wing was ripped off just outboard of the engine. The fuselage and its remaining wing spun clockwise and downward into a narrow gorge that was now visible through the overcast, had there been anyone to see it. The plane, still more or less upright, lost its left wing against the left wall of the gorge and dropped belly-first into the narrow cleft which formed the banks and bed of a rocky stream at the bottom of the canyon. There it remained, wedged in the cleft 30 feet above the stream, hanging by its wing stubs.

CHAPTER 1

ANCHORAGE, ALASKA
SUMMER 1973

She Done Good!

It was late evening but the sun was still well above the horizon. I had just finished watching the Channel Two late news and was preparing to wander out to my back yard with a cup of reheated coffee to watch the sunset. This time of the year it would be a long drawn out affair— I often took an owner's pride in occupying a lawn chair on my small stone patio and watching the ever-changing palette of colors mix and flow over the Alaska Range. The patio was embedded in the rocky soil of a high bluff behind my Anchorage hillside home, and provided an uninterrupted view of the western ranges.

My name is Ben Hunnicutt, retired Major of Artillery, and now—by my own choice—a permanently unemployed Alaskan loafer who occasionally courts trouble by taking on difficult or dangerous jobs for so-called friends.

I had hardly settled myself when, to my annoyance, the crunch of tires from my driveway told me I had a late visitor. Late visitors usually brought trouble of some sort, so I sat quietly, hoping that I would shortly hear a similar departing crunch.

Instead, I heard the familiar and very welcome voice of Elise Nichole.

"Goofing off again, Ben? Staring at the sunset when you should be improving your mind by watching Johnny Carson."

"Don't put Johnny down," I said. "He's the best of them. At least his jokes are funny. Those other TV late night shows have guests whose only claim to fame is being guests on late night shows.

"What are you doing out this late at night, Liz? I thought you were a nice old-fashioned girl."

She came up behind me and delivered an over-the-shoulder kiss, spilling my cooling coffee onto the stone deck.

"You didn't need the coffee anyway. I brought champagne. We're celebrating because I got this today, and I couldn't sleep without sharing it."

Liz was a medium tall brown-eyed brunette with high-sculptured cheekbones that gave her rounded face an exotic touch. She had a coke-bottle figure that suited me fine, though not quite as fashionable as the current fad toward boniness.

She settled in the other lawn chair and handed me a large official-looking packet. While I was opening it, she uncorked a champagne bottle, produced, and filled a pair of plastic wine glasses.

When I finally fumbled the packet open, I saw an elaborately written commendation from the Director of the Federal Bureau of Investigation citing one Special Agent Elise Nichole for outstanding performance of duty in leading an armed raiding party into the remote mountains of Alaska. The success of this operation directly contributed to an equally successful subsequent raid which aided and benefited a valued ally of our nation. The commendation continued in the usual verbose style of such documents, ending with the note that this action would certainly be noted when Agent Nichole was considered for future promotion or special assignments.

If I had known the implications of that final sentence, I'd probably have burned the packet in the stone fireplace before me.

When I handed it back, Liz replaced it with champagne and we drank a silent toast to her achievement.

"Ben, I can't believe this really happened. Most agents might get something like this from lower levels of the FBI, but an 'attaboy' from the Director is really something special. I feel like I'm floating on air. Did you feel like this when you got your Distinguished Service Cross?"

"Not really. I was pumped up, naturally. But in the military, with all the paperwork and verification required, you don't usually get the medal for years after the action. The immediacy is gone, and sometimes you don't even remember the details of what you did. I'm glad the FBI did this for you while it was still fresh."

"It really should have gone to you," she said. "You took the bullet. In fact, it was a group affair—you set it up, you got shot, the bear did his share, and the girl, Nhan, took care of the bad guy. And you figured out how the gold was hidden."

"But you furnished a warm lap for my head, and a cool hand for my brow. Liz, I'll never forget opening my eyes and seeing you looking down at me. If every shot-up soldier could look forward to that, there'd be commendations flying all over the place."

I took her in my arms. Conversation ceased for some minutes, and we left the champagne to itself as we walked arm-in-arm back up to the house.

CHAPTER 2

Shipping Out

It was on a Wednesday afternoon some six weeks later that Liz unexpectedly appeared at my front door. I had just finished cutting what little grass my rocky lawn would support, and was about to dive into a beer, then into the shower. I was definitely not groomed for feminine companionship.

"Well, howdy," I said as I opened the front door. "I wasn't expecting such pretty company. C'mon in."

She stretched up and kissed a sweaty, unshaven cheek, then entered and took a chair at the kitchen table.

"Finish whatever you were up to," she said. "I'll fix us a drink."

I went back and sluiced off, pulled on cleaner jeans, and joined her in the kitchen. I had to wonder what was on her mind—showing up on a work day was not like the duty-bound FBI agent I knew and loved, and a drink before quitting time was even less so. Agent Elise Nichole, while less rigid in her standards than most of her contemporaries, had always been pretty well by-the-book. I walked up behind her chair, buried my face in her neck, and wrapped my arms around her for a deep snuggle. The tenseness I encountered told me to cut it short—I moved around the table and sat, glancing at the drinks she had poured for us.

"The good scotch," I remarked. "This must be an occasion?"

"An occasion, yes. A memorable occasion, yes. An occasion to celebrate—not so much. Ben, I'm being transferred out of Alaska."

I sat transfixed. It was as though someone had walked up and informed me that the world would come to an end at 8:53 tomorrow morning. There was no intelligent response available, just a feeble attempt to absorb and evaluate the information I had just received.

"No chance...?" I began, but she was shaking her head as I stuttered to a stop.

"The Bureau is like the Army, Ben. You stay too long on one station, they figure you'll get stale, quit learning. It's 1973 now. I've been here since '67. A five-year tour is more than most of us get, and the main reason I've been here longer is the good results I got on those cases where we worked together."

"So, where will you be going?" I had finally got enough of my brain in gear to ask a sensible question.

"There's a new science being developed for law enforcement that compares the psychological and lifestyle characteristics of serial criminals that commit certain types of crimes. It's supposed to help narrow a field of suspects by comparing their profiles to those of thousands of known offenders in the data base. It has a long fancy name, but we call it just 'profiling'. I'm being sent to the FBI Behavioral Sciences Division in Quantico for a long course of instruction on the subject. After that, I'll be sent on wherever they need me."

We sat in silence, gazing at each other, neither able to come up with suitable comment or question. Finally, we simultaneously stood and fell into an embrace, standing locked in each other's arms for a full minute before moving to the living room sofa and collapsing in emotional turmoil.

"No options?" I asked, knowing the answer.

"The same option you had when the Army sent down orders. Comply or submit your resignation."

"And I don't reckon you'd consider...?"

"Did you?"

"No, but I was career Army. The service had to come first. You could..."

I stopped just before committing the ultimate error of suggesting that the Bureau was less important to her than the Army had been to me. Her expression told me that I had stopped just in time.

"I won't ask you to leave Alaska and come with me," she said.

"I know you spent 15 years trying to get back here, and I know how much you love this place. There's no way you'd be happy in the lower 48, and I'd be miserable watching you be miserable."

I was inwardly relieved to hear this last; I knew that the possibility of my leaving the state to follow her had to come up, and I knew I'd feel like a self-centered ass if I tried to put into words what Liz had just so clearly expressed. And I knew she had said it first to prevent my having to do so, then feeling like a stinker afterward.

Liz was set to depart two weeks from the day she had informed me of the transfer. She was caught up in the usual complications of a change of station while in government service. These were distracting enough that, while we got together often, we never seemed to get around to discussing the personal and painful aspects of our imminent parting. Finally, we arranged one last evening at my place, rehashing old memories, adventures, and what-if's, and avoiding any speculation about the future.

In the morning, Liz quietly left our bed. I lay in her lingering warmth, pretending sleep; she pretended to believe me. She gathered her belongings, and silently moved out of my life.

CHAPTER 3

Boom Town

Days were long after Liz left. I had previously settled into a routine of bachelor living, doing whatever struck my fancy during the day and seeing Liz occasionally during the week and most weekends. Without the latter to look forward to, hunting, fishing, or exploring the mountains became a drudgery of sameness. I was bored, and I was discovering the true meaning of loneliness. It was hard to forget Liz when, for years, we had shared every special moment, good and bad. Now, every mountain panorama, every sunset, every sight of a newborn moose calf, every small personal victory, carried a reminder that she was not here to share it.

I had always been, to a certain extent, a loner. It wasn't that I deliberately avoided the company of others— just that I didn't constantly need it. My father and I had spent many solitary hours on a lake or a fishing stream, often without needing to exchange a word for hours at a time. He used to say if a man spends time with only himself for company, he'll get to know himself better. And, if he finds he can't stand his own company, how can he expect anyone else to? Now, I was finding myself eating out more, hoping to run into a friend or acquaintance, or wandering down to a gun store or boatyard looking for conversation.

It was late 1973, and Alaska was overflowing with construction companies, pipeline workers, oil field specialty outfits—and gamblers, business girls, con artists, strip joints, and sleazy politicians. The unions were having a field day, as there were large rewards available to anyone who could finagle a high-paying construction camp job or a lucrative construction contract for some newly discovered friend with connections. The big oil companies were willing to spend whatever it took to get the pipeline and its associated camps built, and to start the oil flowing—and they did.

Liquor, dope, and cash flowed freely along the sidewalks of Anchorage, and there were many to profit from the demand. There were more than enough women to help the big spenders spend, and spend they did.

Men worked 12 hours a day for weeks or months on end, drawing overtime and double time, and making a normal year's pay in a month. When their tours were done, some went back to families in the States, banked their money, and awaited their next tour. Others headed straight for Anchorage, Fairbanks, or other familiar cities, pouring their pay into the many money-pits made available to them by local entrepreneurs.

When a construction stiff was sucked dry of his last paycheck, a call to the union hall generally resulted in a new summons to fill a fresh vacancy, one which just happened to fit his qualifications.

Although the first section of pipe had yet to be laid, an 800 plus mile route had to be surveyed, physically and geologically, and several dozen work camps constructed—camps capable of supporting, feeding, and billeting several hundred men (and some women) in a wilderness where the sudden lack of heat, shelter, or medical facilities could mean quick death. The road connecting and supplying these camps had to be built as the camps were built, and built over muskeg and mountain, through forests and swamp, and across river systems whose beds, channels, and direction changed from season to season.

The similarity of Anchorage to old western cattle-shipping towns, such as Abilene and Dodge City, was evident—if not in appearance, in attitude. Freshly paid oil patch hands hit town with the same pent-up desires as the earlier cow hands, and found the same classes of parasites waiting to fulfill them. The big difference, one enforced by pipeline companies intent on keeping their skilled employees in good health, was that the suckers now came unarmed. Since the parasites had no such restrictions, muggings and occasional murders kept the play lively.

The police, among whom I had a few friends, handled the rougher situations well, but could in no way control the thousands of prostitutes and "B" girls who descended upon the city like bees to a honey pot. Many were pros from the west coast or Las Vegas; they usually came complete with their pimps and protectors, and with enough connections to be safe from the law.

College girls began to show up from the lower 48; their specialties leaned more toward dancing in the many strip clubs than to street work. A girl's nightly tips, usually hundred-dollar bills tucked into what little she wore on stage, could equal a semester's tuition. And some of the more liberal colleges might even award her credit for social research—or so I was told by a California-based researcher who studied at the Great Alaska Bush Company.

The professional ladies were usually kept safe by their associates, and most of the dancers seemed able to keep problems at an arm's length.

But there was a victim class which was less fortunate. Native women from remote villages, barely mature girls from the States, young runaways, "ruined" girls looking for a new start, newly-hooked addicts with a habit to feed—all had heard of the fabulous fortunes to be made from the Alaska oil-rush. Of this class, few had the real-world experience needed to safely navigate a sea of greedy predators and human sharks.

It was from among these amateurs that the first casualties came. A girl would be beaten and raped, perhaps found in a Fourth Avenue alley. The crime would be reported, and would go "into the books", but the likelihood of identifying and apprehending the criminal was slim. The number of such reported cases slowly grew, and a few perpetrators actually identified and caught.

But a more insidious trend eventually came to light—the complete disappearance of some of the solo operators. Unless a friend reported her absence, a street or bar girl could evaporate into thin air without being missed. It was common enough for a girl to decide to go home, or to take a steady boyfriend and leave the street, or to change her name and try working Fairbanks for a change. Or be murdered and buried in a shallow grave. No one would notice.

Finally, amid a number of reports of disappearances and several botched attempts at kidnapping, the authorities realized that one or more sexual predators were actually trolling for victims along the streets of Anchorage. According to my police contacts, an unofficial task force was working to identify a possible serial killer. When four women's bodies turned up in places as diversified as Turnagain Arm, the Knik River flats, and the Eklutna road, a serious hunt began. When ballistic tests showed that several of the victims had been killed with the same weapon, a quiet but intense manhunt began and the FBI was asked to help.

CHAPTER 4

Chasing a Star

Summer and fall had gone. The winter of '74 seemed a bit greyer and bleaker than normal. I would have sworn that the average temperature had dropped 10 degrees when Liz left town.

I had pretty well stayed clear of the gambling and drinking that pervaded the livelier sections of Anchorage. Not that I was all that puritanical, but as a young soldier I had dumped my pay into some of the more notorious cesspools of the world. Once you've seen the fleshpots of the far-east, Anchorage's Fourth Avenue is pretty tame. And, I had to admit, frequenting the bars or the girlie shows seemed like self-torture—like standing outside a bakery and smelling the fresh doughnuts when you were hungry and broke.

It was a little distressing to see my Anchorage, which I had always thought of as a nice little city with a small-town complex, turning into a honky-tonk town. I often wondered how much of the money that was rolling in to our city would actually stay there.

I began looking for excuses to leave the noise, stress, and crime, and to get back to the mountains and bush for a while. Cooper Landing served as an escape hatch during the spring, and I enjoyed the company of the regulars at Bill Fuller's gun shop. When his range was clear of snow, targets were set up and the projects we had nursed through the winter months were tested under the critical eyes of our expert gunsmiths, Bill, and John. My own pet was an 1873 Springfield rifle dating from the Indian Wars which I had converted to a long-range target rifle. It performed beyond my expectations, probably because John had selected and fitted the custom barrel in his hillside shop. But after several weeks of burning powder and listening to its 40 caliber slugs consistently ring the 550-yard ram target, I became bored and somewhat restless.

I spent a week in Seward visiting with Gary and Nina Brandt, and renewing acquaintance with their young son Jody, now six and full of energy and questions. One of his questions unfortunately had to do with the whereabouts of Liz, so I had to update the Brandts. I made it short, and they immediately changed the subject, much to my relief.

Gary Brandt was a giant of a man, six and a half feet of well-tuned muscle and a shock of blonde hair like a Viking chief. He worked for the Alaska Railroad on weekly shifts, and I had caught him on an off-work week. The weather was good and Gary knew the flounder holes, so we spent a pleasant few days on the water. Jody was becoming an accomplished waterman in his own right, and took pride in teaching me the tricks and techniques passed to him by his proud father.

Nina Brandt's sister, Dora, had been murdered along with her fiancé, Joe Doane, one of my first recruits in the stay-behind-agent operation formerly known as Operation Washtub. Gary and I had worked together to confirm the murders, and to try to identify the killer. Liz and I had eventually tracked him down and taken him out of play, but it had been a very close call as to who would eliminate whom.

The Brandts and I had remained close friends since that time, and I was particularly taken with young Jody. As sturdy as his Viking father, but with a gentle side inherited from his mother, Jody set the pattern for what I hoped any son of mine might become.

Not wishing to overstay my welcome, and with my restlessness becoming obvious to my hosts, I loaded my truck and returned to Anchorage and my place off Rabbit Creek Road.

It was during a lunch at Peggy's restaurant, where I had hoped I'd run into Mike Gearhart, that I fell into a conversation with Wil Allison, a hunting guide and bush pilot who operated out of the Nebesna area. He was telling a fellow pilot that he thought he might have found a clue to the location of a wrecked WW2 airplane. My ears perked up immediately—I had always had a bit of treasure hunting in my makeup, and searching out a war relic sounded interesting enough to take my mind off my troubles. I asked Wil if he was going to hunt for the plane. He laughed.

"Most of those rumors don't turn out. Any other time, I'd probably take a quick look, but I'm booked up solid with hunting clients, and I need to cash in on 'em while the weather's good. Why don't you chase it down, Ben? You're a man of leisure, and you can handle yourself in the bush."

I thought about the matter through a cup of lukewarm coffee.

"I don't want to jump your claim, Wil. If I discovered something of value, it could turn into some kind of personal hassle. You can always check it out after the guiding season is over."

"Ben, as soon as the season is over, I'm headin' to Hawaii for about six weeks of sun and girl watching. Maybe longer, depending on how things work out. If you want to chase down that wreck, have at it. If it's fulla gold, I'll cheer for you and you can buy me a drink sometime.

"Here's what little I know," he continued. "Old Native guy I ran into in a bar in Fairbanks was talking about prospecting up in the Gerstle River country. He mentioned an odd narrow pass through a mountain chain. I recognized it—had thought I was the only one that knew about it, so I started listening. Said it was a narrow gorge, so choked with rocks, trees, and debris that you couldn't get through on foot. He panned the stream as far up it as he could get, and gave up.

"He said he noticed an old airplane wreck wedged in between the rock walls of the gorge. Couldn't get up to it to check it out for valuables, so said the hell with it; went back to the river and panned his way back to the highway."

"No guess as to what kind of plane?" I asked.

"Only said it had a star on it. That means it's probably military, but it could be anything. Did say it was brown in color—might mean olive drab."

"Well," I said, "if it's a fighter, like a P-39 or P-63, it's sure worth salvaging. If it's just a cargo plane, not so much. Maybe I could get in there and check it out, and we could go from there."

"What's this 'we'? I told you I'm outta here right after I convince that last Texas millionaire that he just killed a record sheep. I'll plot it on a map for you, and I can set you down on the east end of the pass while I'm resupplying one of my hunting camps. Once you cross the chain and find—or don't find—the wreck, you'll have to take care of getting yourself back. I'll be exploring Hawaiian wildlife at close range."

Remembering Wil Allison's reputation as a lady-chaser, I believed him. I asked a few more questions and agreed to fly north with him when he left Anchorage. I then contacted a bush pilot I had used previously, Red Buckner, and made arrangements for a pickup two days after I calculated I should have finished the trek through the valley. The pickup would have to be on floats according to Wil, as the stream forming the bottom of the pass emerged into a large shallow lake. I gave Red a map which Wil had annotated with what I fervently hoped was all the information he would need to find me.

CHAPTER 5

If One Must Fly

I spent the next few days getting my gear into shape and picking up the food I would need to get me through. I went light, minimal food—mostly super light-weight LRP Rations, called "Lurp Rats" by the GIs. The LRP rations (Long Range Patrol) were furnished by a friend in the military. A good sleeping bag, extra warm outer gear, my loaded 338 rifle and a spare box of 20 rounds added to the load. I was out of condition, but figured keeping my pack under 45 pounds would compensate. A very lightweight tarp to serve as a crude tent, and a quart water bottle completed my outfit. My lucky Smith & Wesson snub-nosed 38 rode in an outer jacket pocket— I always felt a bit more comfortable when it was handy.

I had breakfast with Allison at Peggy's on the appointed day, as excited as a kid headed to Boy Scout camp. We went over my plan again, making sure I knew all he could tell me about the area I was to explore. I restrained my desire for coffee refills—there's no lavatory in a Cessna 185—and handed him a note with info as to who to notify in case I didn't show up again. Liz was not on it.

I watched Wil do his pre-flight check, pleased with the serious attention he gave it. Many pilots settled for a perfunctory walk-around, checking only the things they considered important—I had been out on crash-search parties for a few of the more careless ones. I wanted anyone who was flying me to do a lot more than counting the wings and checking gas and oil. I don't care for flying, and do so only when there is no other reasonable means of transport.

It was a fine day for it, if one feels one must fly. Wil took us off from Merrill Field, banked around to the northeast, and generally followed the Glenn Highway toward Glennallen. I was thankful that the air was smooth, at least at this point. I knew the country we were flying over and enjoyed the different perspective afforded by the aerial view. As we passed by the Matanuska Glacier and on over the Eureka area, I strained to see the valley containing the Little Nel gold mine where I had got shot up rescuing two Vietnamese human trafficking victims just summer before last. The valley was apparently hidden by its surrounding hills, but my memories suddenly sharpened into focus. Memories not so much of the incident or of the pain of the bullet slicing through my chest—but of regaining consciousness with my head cradled in Liz's warm lap, and her hand stroking my brow. I jerked my mind back to the present. I had gone days without feeling sorry for myself. This was no time to start.

When we swung north from Glennallen, we entered territory unfamiliar to me. This was the country that Wil Allison had travelled and hunted for decades, and I had to put my faith in his knowledge and instincts. I tried to trace our journey on the map I had brought along, but the contours of the land below didn't seem to match those on the piece of paper in my hand. I eventually gave up, trusting that Wil would orient me after we landed.

I was awakened from an involuntary nap by a few jabs from the pilot. He pointed to a postage stamp-sized smooth spot on a sandbar below us.

"That's where I'll put you off," he shouted. He then flew toward a deep cleft in a mountain range about a half mile from the landing strip, descended a thousand feet, and took a course across the range, paralleling the narrow gorge which bisected the range. The gorge cut through the hills at a place where the range narrowed considerably before widening again further south.

We flew the length of the narrow pass until it broke out on the west side of the mountain mass, a distance of possibly eight or ten miles. The depths of the pass were in shadow, and probably remained so all year round; I was never able to get a glimpse of the bottom. Where the pass finally exited into a river valley, the stream widened out into a shallow lake about a mile long and half as wide. As we circled the lake, I looked for gravel bars that might be suitable for a wheeled landing. An old glacial moraine and many scattered boulders disrupted the flood plain to the point that only a helicopter pilot or a very optimistic Super Cub jockey would try to land.

The mouth of the gorge was marked by a heavy growth of brush and small trees where the stream had dumped nutrients within reach of the sun. Back beyond the brush was heavy shadow, the sun blocked by the steep valley walls. I had given Red Buckner a map on which Wil had marked this spot and added notes to help locate it. Circling here, imagining myself alone, stranded, and running out of food, I hoped Wil and Red spoke the same language.

"If your guy stands you up," said Wil, reading my mind, "head north." He jabbed a thumb in a northerly direction.

"All the rivers and major streams around here run north, and you're bound to hit the Alaska Highway sooner or later if you live."

He banked the plane around and flew us back over the pass to the gravel patch on the east end that served as a landing strip. The landing was good enough, I supposed, but bumpy—hollow sounding "clunks" reverberating throughout the fuselage had me wondering what essential part was about to fall off. He taxied us as close to the mouth of the gorge as possible and shut down the engine. As soon as the propeller had jerked to a stop, I was out of the plane answering an urgent call of nature. When finished I turned to the plane to unload my gear and I saw Wil watering the petunias under the opposite wing. I could see that flying around the country in a small plane could involve unusual logistical problems.

Wil helped me haul my gear to a sheltered camping spot near where the stream entered the narrow pass.

"Well, Ben, good luck to you. If you find anything, think twice before letting the world know. There're people out there who'd fly in here and strip a wreck to bare bones while you're trying to figure how to get it out. And if it's a former government airplane, there could be a lot of questions as to ownership. Do your homework before you brag.

"And if you would," he added, "help me walk this strip and

clear away any snags, rocks bigger than a grapefruit, and anything else that could cause problems on landing or takeoff."

We spent a half hour doing so before Wil fired up the Cessna, waved farewell, and took off. I stood, listened as the sound of his departure faded away, and felt like the only person left in the world.

I decided to camp here for the night and get an early start in the morning. The weather was clear, and, for now, warm; the weather experts had predicted little change for the next four to five days. My camp wasn't much—a fire for tradition's sake, the tarp pegged down to form a floor, bent and propped toward the fire to make a crude reflector, and the sleeping bag stretched out in the "V". Chow was to be two cans of chili, the heaviest rations I had brought along. By eating them now, I'd have a good meal under my belt when I started out, and there would be that much less weight to carry in my pack. The LRP rations furnished instant coffee and the stream plentiful water. I dined in some comfort, took a walk to settle things down, and crawled into my sleeping bag hoping to sleep early and long.

I slept neither. My mind running through the what-ifs of the job ahead took care of the early—a noisy porcupine, grunting and poking his nose into my belongings scared the hell out of me and took care of the long.

CHAPTER 6

The Canyon

'Liz is gone.'
I savagely thrust the thought from my mind and looked out over the narrow valley which confronted me. This wasn't just another valley in a land where mountains, hills, and valleys made up most of the landscape. It was like a cruel deep knife slash, severing the spine of the mountain chain I was trying to cross. The left wall of the valley was nearly vertical, while the right wall was laid back at about a 45-degree angle. A simple traverse, I thought, side-hilling the right wall, staying well above the debris choked stream in the narrow gorge below. This avoided both the high peaks, some still snow tipped, which rimmed the valley, and the narrow debris-choked cleft below. A hard day's walk should put me on the other end of the valley and across the mountain range.

Not that I would have cared very much had I been forced to take a more difficult route. My mood was less than cheerful today; thoughts of Liz intruded and I found myself moving carelessly, ignoring the small necessary safeguards of a seasoned mountain traveler—not bothering to slowly test a rock before trusting it with my full weight, neglecting to stop and evaluate each small segment of the route before committing to it, and not stopping every few minutes to familiarize myself with newly revealed terrain.

The latter was undoubtedly the reason I suddenly realized, after hours of side-hilling on reasonably firm ground, that I was fifty yards out into an old slide area, crossing a field of small boulders ranging from small scree to beach-ball sized chunks. The last rock I had put my weight upon, about the size of a watermelon, had slid from under my downhill foot. I fell on my right side, grinding my slung rifle into the dirt, and watched the dislodged rock as it tumbled down the slope, picking up others until it formed its own mini-avalanche and crashed into the trees and brush at the bottom of the gorge.

After a few moments of mentally chewing myself out, I brushed off my rifle and checked the scope for damage. All seemed OK, but the newly refurbished stock was no longer like new. I made sure the chamber was still empty and the magazine full. The boulder field appeared to be quite wide and extended nearly to the top of the valley wall. Not wanting to waste time and energy climbing to a point above the slide, I resolved to continue my crossing—but more carefully. I cinched my pack tight, not wanting to risk losing it in another fall and having to chase it down into the dark gorge below.

Another dozen or so more carefully taken steps loosened a smaller rock which, following the inexorable law of gravity, bounced its way downslope. It fell with less fuss than the first, cracked against an unseen mate buried in the vegetation below and came to rest somewhere under the tangled mass of dead trees, avalanche debris and root wads that filled the bottom of the gorge. It dawned on me that few of the giant stepping stones I had put my trust in were securely bedded. If I weren't more cautious, I could easily become a part of a self-made avalanche and end up trying to ride a rock down the chute and into the gorge feet below.

I continued across the boulder patch, hunkered low now so I could sprawl wide and anchor myself in case a key rock gave way and left me scrabbling for a solid surface. An hour later, I stopped for a breather and took stock of the 50 or so yards remaining between me and relatively solid terrain. The surface around me was different somehow, more uneven with larger rocks exposed. As I took the next tentative step, another melon-sized rock skittered from underfoot and began its merry way down the mountain. I held up and watched it go—it was actually fascinating to see these several hundred-pound boulders leaping and bounding down the hill, crashing into others like monstrous billiard balls and plunging out of sight into the intermingled mass of stone and vegetation at the bottom. Either the final crack of rock against rock, or a cushioned thump, would indicate whether or not the boulder had made its way to the stream bed.

I needed to be more careful. 'Liz would give you hell,' I thought to myself, 'gallivanting around live rock slides like a damn amateur, nobody even knowing where to look for the body if you screw up.'

'LIZ IS GONE!' my mind shouted back. 'There's nobody else gives a damn! Just get to work and finish this trek.'

I boldly stepped out like I was on a downtown sidewalk and made another dozen strides before sending another large boulder crashing down the slope. I stopped and watched its course as it zig-zagged its way downward, finally ricocheting off an embedded outcropping and shooting off into the gorge at an angle. I awaited the sound of its final impact, mildly curious as to whether or not it would strike the bottom, or hang up in the vegetation.

To my surprise, the sound echoing up from the bottom of the canyon was neither crack nor crash, but a dull metallic clank.

I wondered if I had heard the clank or imagined it—I found another similar sized stone and booted it off in the direction of the first. Naturally, it bounced off in a different direction and crashed into the brush below, clankless. I moved forward 20 yards or so and sent several other stony messengers down the grade. One seemed to follow the path of the first and I eventually heard a distinct metallic impact, as though it had struck an old 55-gallon oil drum.

I hauled out my binoculars, sat down, and carefully glassed the gully where the rocks had disappeared. Nothing man-made was visible from where I sat, and the deep shadow below indicated that nothing was likely to be. If I went down to check the area out and there was nothing, I'd have to climb back up the valley wall to continue on my way. If I found some old mining junk or oil drums, I'd have to cuss like a drunk Marine and still climb back out. If I found the wrecked airplane, I'd have to climb back out, or spend the night in a dark, cold, wet cleft in the rocky bottom of the valley. Climbing out seemed a part of every option.

Looking ahead along the valley, I could see the valley walls falling away as the pass ended and opened onto the flood plain and the lake. I mentally marked the suspect spot below as well as I could and proceeded along the slope to the end of the slide area. I was encouraged when an unintentionally dislodged boulder danced its way down the hill and struck near the spot I had marked, sending up another unmistakable clang. A sign of luck perhaps?

A nice camp site and a good meal where the stream emerged from the valley, a night of rest for my weary legs, and I'd be ready to approach the wreck, if there was one, from its own level.

CHAPTER 7

The Wreck

    I found my camping spot near where the mouth of the stream exited the gorge, set up camp, selected a LRP Ration that didn't seem too inedible, and planned the next morning's strategy. Rethinking the matter, charging into that dark canyon on the strength of a few clanks and clangs didn't seem all that bright. It was very possible that some oil drums or mining machinery could have been washed down the gorge during a spring flood decades ago. I decided to retrace my path along the valley wall to the spot I had marked, but at a much lower level. If I could spot the source of those metallic noises while on a relatively easy traverse low on the mountain, I would either save a bunch of unnecessary bushwhacking, or justify the intense labor to come.

    After the day's trek, I had little trouble sleeping, and if any of the local critters toured my camp during the night, they didn't disturb me. A packet of rehydrated beans served as breakfast. I knew they were beans because the outside of the packet was so marked—without the label to guide me, I'd never have guessed.

    I left the heavier part of my load in camp and backtracked to the canyon wall, climbed just high enough to clear the bottom growth, and worked my way to the spot I had marked in my mind. Dragging out my binoculars, I sat on a convenient rock, unfortunately not yet warmed by the sun, and meticulously examined every visible foot of the gorge below.

    After nearly 20 minutes of this rather boring exercise, my butt beginning to feel as though it was frozen to the rock, I lowered the binocs to give my eyes a few minutes of rest. As my eyes refocused, a memory flash of something "not quite right" rang a bell and I whipped the glass up and rechecked the area I had last examined.

A spot of red, too red to be natural. A dull red on a patch of brown. It just didn't look right. I moved a few yards to get a view from a different angle, and it leaped out at me. I was looking at a fragment of a red star painted on a dull brown airplane wing. A wing from a multi-engine aircraft, obviously, as the engine nacelle was partly visible from my new angle.

I moved around to view the wing from other angles—it was just a wing, a left wing, no other aircraft parts were in evidence. It was mostly sheltered from view by the residue of dozens of storms, floods, and small rock falls over the years. Dirt, gravel, and possibly some of the rocks that had produced the clanking sound, were scattered over the olive drab upper surface. The flaking, peeling red star which had first caught my eye had faded nearer to orange-pink, a white background showing under it in spots.

OK, I now knew that there was definitely a wrecked plane in the vicinity, and I knew its origin. Of course, the remainder of the aircraft could be a mountain or two away—or a hundred yards farther down the gorge. I could only hope it was nearby, and that I could find it in the time remaining for my search.

As to the origin, I knew that, during WW2, the United States had initiated a lend-lease program for Russia which sent hundreds of US planes through Alaska and on to Siberia and Stalingrad. Both fighters and bombers were sent, as well as cargo planes loaded with war material and supplies to help the Russians beat back the German invaders. The planes were ferried to Great Falls, Montana, where they were inspected and officially accepted by Russian authorities. Red stars, the official Russian air force insignia, were painted over the original US Air Corps markings.

Most were then flown on to Ladd Field near Fairbanks, Alaska, by American ferry pilots. There, they were taken over by Russian ferry crewmen and flown to Nome and on into Siberia and to Russia.

This was obviously a light bomber or cargo plane that had lost its way and gone down while inbound or outbound from Ladd

Field. All I had to do now was find the rest of it, determine if it could be salvaged, or if it was worth salvaging, manage to get home and pull together an interested recovery crew.

I was beginning to think that it would have to be loaded with gold or jewels to make this expedition worthwhile. I was in my early forties, heavier than I should be, and a lot more out of shape than I should be; the hike so far had taken a lot more out of me than I wanted to admit.

I worked my way back to the comfort of level ground and returned to my camp around noon. I had intended to take the remainder of the day to rest and to make a final search up the canyon mouth tomorrow after a good night's sleep, but nagging thoughts about the possible whereabouts of the main part of the wreck chipped away at my brain.

Finally, after a snack and an hour's refreshing nap, I loaded myself up again, still in the light-pack mode and struck out for the darkly forbidding outlet of the gorge. The stream was shallow, and it was easy to cross back and forth as necessary to find decent footing. Fifteen minutes of careful travel found me about 200 yards up the stream, walking in the near-twilight caused by the lack of both sun and visible sky, and by the tangle of dead trees and live greenery jammed in the bottom of the gorge. I had just stopped to rest, and to look up at the slim streak of blue sky visible from the depths of the narrow valley, when I found myself staring at a long muddy-brown torpedo-shaped object suspended some 30 or more feet directly above me. I backed up a few yards to gain a different perspective and was able to see the flight deck windows and windshield of a C-47 cargo aircraft. From this angle I could see that it was not really suspended above me, but was firmly wedged between opposing rock walls by the stubs of what had been its sheared-off wings.

I dropped my pack, leaned my rifle against a convenient boulder, and regarded the plane. The fuselage appeared intact, even the cabin windows unbroken. I moved toward the tail section and noted that the large cargo door on the left side was still securely closed. I could see no evidence of any opening in the body of the airplane. My mind unwillingly reached a conclusion that caused me to shiver a bit—the crew had to still be aboard.

I studied the plane intently, trying to devise some means of access. It became obvious that I'd have to scale the bluff on my left and try to make my way onto the remains of the right wing. If I could crawl toward the main fuselage, I might be able to look through one of the small windows and determine the condition of the interior and the flight cabin. If I slipped and fell off, I'd probably spend a very long time lying in a stream in the middle of nowhere with broken bones.

The main cargo door was on the opposite side of the plane, but the canyon wall on that side was solid rock and nearly straight up. There was no chance I'd be able to climb it and get to that door. And, I reminded myself, the force of the crash had to have distorted the fuselage to the point that the cargo door was likely to be jammed in its recess—not openable by an easy turn of the lever.

I gave up for the day. A fresh start tomorrow might bring new ideas and a fresh approach. I was tired enough that I decided to forgo the Lurp, settling for a large candy bar instead, and crawling into the sack not long after.

CHAPTER 8

A Guest for Breakfast

I dreamed that a group of Russian airmen came into my camp and asked for help in getting their plane down so they could fly it home to Russia. I tried to explain that first we'd have to find the other wing, but they insisted that they had a good pilot and he could get them home on one wing. As I was mulling over the problem, I gradually became awake and aware of a snuffling sound behind my makeshift tent.

I wormed out of my sleeping bag, grasped the stock of my rifle, and slowly stood to peer over the half-tent. I expected to see the brother of the porcupine which had awakened me several mornings before; what I did see in the early morning light was a large glossy-furred black bear, standing erect and staring back at me over the tent wall. Without thinking, I threw up my arms and roared as loudly as I could, directly into the bear's face. Realizing instantly that the bear might take that as a challenge, I levelled the rifle and cranked a round into the chamber.

Whatever I might have had to do after that, I would have been far too late— before the bolt was even closed, the bear almost fell over in surprise, spun around, and launched itself like a racehorse toward the nearest tree cover. I stood without moving, the tension gradually draining from my mind and body as the adrenal surge spent itself. After I had sat down on a log I had dragged into camp for that purpose, I remembered that I had chambered a cartridge in the 338. In light of my recent experience with an uninvited visitor, I decided to leave the rifle loaded and ready, but with the safety engaged. Had the bear been a grizzly in a bad mood, I would never have had time to work the bolt and shoot.

I really hadn't intended to be up so early, but there was no easy path back to slumber after my encounter with the bear. I dug out a Lurp Rat labelled 'chicken stew' and decided to give it a try. I ripped away the thick outer cover of tough non-reflective OD paper and dumped the accessory packet to get at the instant coffee. Maxwell House this time, I noted with pleasure—some of the off-brand coffee packets that turned up in Lurps and MRE's were not all that palatable. None was as bitter, however, as the coffee in packets from the old Korean War C-Rations; I wouldn't complain now.

The meal itself was freeze dried and vacuum packed in a heavy foil bag with instructions printed thereon. The instructions, which I didn't usually take the time to read, stated that one could eat the contents dry if necessary, rather than adding the prescribed half canteen cup of water. Curious, I tried a pinch of the dry granules on my tongue. Like salty cereal, I noted, but without any taste of chicken. I added the requisite cup of hot water, stirred vigorously with the plastic spoon from the accessory pack, and began to eat—assuming that the water would bring out the taste. More like salty oatmeal, but the chicken flavor, if it had ever existed, had long since escaped. I finished it, more out of duty than of hunger, and settled for the pair of chocolate discs from the packet. I washed them down with instant coffee cut with powdered cream substitute.

When I awoke from what was intended to be a short nap, the sun was finally far enough around to the west to throw some light into the gorge. Having been bothered by neither Russians nor bears, I'd slept much longer than intended. Gathering what gear I thought I might need, I headed back to the C-47 hoping to come up with a safe mode of getting a peek into its interior.

I stared at it from its front, waiting for the spark of an idea which didn't want to be born. The old bird stared back, the twin cockpit windshields unblinking, uninviting, and far above my reach. The remnant of its right wing was probably accessible after a somewhat risky climb, but crawling along the rounded aluminum surface toward the fuselage seemed pretty chancy. The plane had settled at a nose-down angle; if the wing surface was the slightest bit slippery, the odds were that I'd slide over its leading edge and to the streambed below. I could see no handholds, just the right engine and its grotesquely bent propeller.

The words of a very able Infantry Lieutenant, uttered in Korea long ago, came into my mind: "There are very few problems which cannot be solved by the judicious application of high explosives." He spoke these words partly in jest, but a quick-witted Sergeant had taken them to heart and had applied them to the destruction of a score of North Korean attackers.

I wondered now if perhaps a few small shaped charges could be used to cut the right wing and engine loose from the body of the airplane and cause it to drop into the stream bed where it could then be accessed.

'Yeah, Stupid,' I thought to myself, 'and how do you get to the wing root to place the charges? If you can get there, you don't need the charges.'

I walked around the C-47 several times, fixing in my mind its attitude and its estimated distances from the ground and canyon walls. I took its tail number, which was mostly visible through the flaking, fading paint applied by its new Russian owners 30 years ago. I wrote down what could be an 8, a 0, or a 3, adding a question mark, followed by 43943. Then I made my way back to my camp, resolved to forgo any foolhardy plan that would risk my injuring myself and not being able to return to civilization. I gathered dead wood and spotted it to trace a large arrow pointing to my campsite, showing Red Buckner where to beach his floatplane after landing on the shallow lake on the Gerstle River flats.

I busied myself for most of the remaining day making notes concerning the location of the C-47 and what equipment might be needed for its entry and salvage, if it came to that. For some reason, it never occurred to me to just report it and leave it unexplored. Not that I expected anything of great value to be inside—I had seen enough military equipment and supplies in my life not to be thrilled by the discovery of more.

The challenge of gaining entry combined with curiosity regarding its contents were my main incentives, plus the nagging thought that those remaining inside—if any—deserved the recognition and honors due to fighting men of any nation.

CHAPTER 9

Steak But No Dessert

Red Buckner's float plane showed up well before noon the next day. Although I had perfect confidence in him, I had to admit to a sense of relief as I waded out and helped beach the machine—there is always the possibility that the only person who knows where you are will crack up on route, and you'll both be marooned in the wilderness until rescue or death.

I had packed my gear and had it ready for stowing except for a tin of hot coffee and a cup. When Red had finished watering the petunias, I poured half the tin into the cup and handed it to him. We perched side-by-side on the sitting log while he sipped away gratefully.

I first met Red when he flew me to a remote luxury fishing lodge for a clandestine meeting with an American intelligence officer. I had been recruited for an undercover investigation which subsequently cost two bad guys their lives and left me with a severe bullet wound. The end result was the freeing of two Vietnamese women from a period of domestic and sexual slavery, and the breaking up of an international gold smuggling ring. I considered it a break-even operation—I was well paid and Liz earned a commendation from her FBI chief. But I could have done without the bullet.

Red had the deep resonant voice of a movie hero, but was only about five feet three inches tall—an incongruity which took some getting used to.

"Hey, Red, I don't think I've ever seen your wife around Lake

Hood. Does she work with your rinky-dink flying circus, or does she have a real job somewhere?"

Red looked at me and cogitated for 30 seconds or so.

"What you really want to know," he said, "is whether she is short like me, or did I marry a woman I have to look up to."

His guess was more or less accurate, and I was embarrassed enough to blush and look away.

"Well, Red," I lied, "I gotta admit I was curious about that too, but the question was real."

"She's about your height", he replied, "but a helluva lot smarter. She runs the office and does the scheduling for the outfit. And," he added, "right now she's the only one in the world who knows exactly where you and I are, so you'd better hope she's happy and in good health."

He stood and threw out his remaining coffee.

"You gonna show me what you found, or didn't you find it?"

"Between us?" I asked.

"Between us."

I picked up my rifle and led him back into the gorge to where the C-47 hung suspended like a museum exhibit. Red looked it over in silence, shaking his head.

"You've got a job of work waiting for you, 'cause I know you won't just report it and leave it there. You're too curious about what's inside. I am too."

He turned back toward camp. "Come on, we better haul ass out of here—there's some weather brewing near the pass over the Matt Glacier and we may have a bumpy ride back."

Red's "may have a bumpy ride" was the understatement of the year. As we passed over Eureka, winds began to toss the little airplane around like a rowboat on a rough sea. My innards, usually invulnerable to the angrier moods of air and ocean, began to protest indignantly. Fortunately, the air smoothed out about the time we crossed the Chickaloon River and I was not obliged to sully my dignity or Red Buckner's airplane.

The remainder of the flight and its landing at Lake Hood were uneventful, and I did get to meet Mrs. Buckner. She met us at the dock and kindly offered me a ride to my truck, still parked at Merrill Field. Red had erred somewhat in his description of his wife's height; she was a good six feet tall, and they made a definite Mutt & Jeff impression as they strode down the dock together. A sharp glance from Red implied that no comment on the matter was either necessary or welcome.

I arrived at home with plenty of time to clean and stow my gear, strip and clean the Winchester, and make a call to the FAA concerning my find of the C-47 wreckage. The person on the other end of the phone didn't seem all that interested, but promised to relay the information to those who might be.

I cleaned myself up, shaved, reclothed, and, timing my trip carefully, drove down the hillside and to the Club Paris, arriving just at 6:00 when the parking meters no longer had to be fed. The place was near full, as usual, and noisy, but I was content to wait at the bar, soaking up a Tanqueray martini until a seat was available. The place was dark and smoky, but living in a man's world, I was accustomed to second-hand smoke—although I did hope that someday smoking might be forbidden in eating establishments.

They soon found me a seat at a small table against the side wall, where I sat and requested a refill on my martini. The replacement drink was brought over by a strikingly pretty dark-haired, high cheek-boned lady who immediately reminded me of Liz, thus spoiling what I had hoped to be a pleasant meal. I ordered the petite filet well done with sautéed mushrooms on the side, with a salad to start. The waitress took my order without using pencil or pad, smiled, and disappeared. I had to admire the servers who worked at the Paris—they made it a point to memorize orders, even from parties of four or five, never writing them down and seldom making mistakes.

I hoped the filet would erase the memory and after-taste of the desiccated combat rations I had been feeding myself lately. As near as I could tell, the only advantage of the Lurp Rats was their feather-lightness—and you still had to carry or find water (which is heavy) to prepare them. Or learn to eat them dry, which would require desperate hunger, at least in my case.

The meal was excellent, as expected, and the waitress seemed more than usually friendly. Her resemblance to Liz was a bit of a turn on, but an immediate feeling of guilt pretty well doused any spark that arose. I had my dinner and left without dessert of any kind.

CHAPTER 10

Yes, I Have No Doorbell

If McGann had come by a week earlier, or a week later, I'd have told him to go to hell. But he didn't—he knocked on my door at a time when I was a little hung over, and a lot feeling sorry for myself. Liz had been gone just over a year, and the loneliness and sense of loss had worn their way through my thin defenses. I was angry at her, at myself, at the FBI, and at anyone who had the bad luck to step into my danger zone.

I ignored the knock and debated whether another beer would be a good idea right now. The knock was repeated after a reasonable wait, so I answered it. Facing me was Jim McGann, an Army Counter-Intelligence Corps agent I had known briefly at OCS, 20-odd years ago. I got to know him more intimately in 1969 when I served as a contract agent for the CIC during a terrorist attempt to abduct a nuclear warhead. We had parted on neutral terms, but I had a strong suspicion that his present appearance at my door presaged trouble of some sort. Well, maybe trouble was what I needed—or deserved. Also, hospitality demanded that I offer my guest a beer, thus providing an excuse for me to have another.

"Jim McGann. Come in. Don't tell me you guys have lost another warhead?"

McGann, apparently wearing the same wrinkled suit in which I had last seen him, offered a perfunctory handshake, slouched over to the sofa and sprawled onto it like a teenager. Jim was a tall gangly person with all the grace of a moose calf, and very unlikely to ever be stereotyped as a secret agent.

"I see you not only disconnected your doorbell; this time you even took the damn' button away. What've you got against doorbells, Ben?"

"Let me get you a beer, Jim, or are you on duty?"

"OK, and yes," he responded. "Just make sure it's not kin to that skull-popper you set me up with last time."

"I'll make it just Moosehead. You can probably handle that if you can figure how to get the cap off."

While I went to the fridge and grabbed a couple of bottles of Canadian Moosehead lager, Jim unwound from the sofa and examined the few photos I displayed on the mantle over the fireplace. He poked a finger at an especially good shot of Liz posed with Pioneer Peak as a background.

"That's one heckuva gal you have, Ben—smart, pretty, and good at her job."

"Had," I muttered shortly, turning away and leading him through the back-sliding door and out to the stone patio which sat on the lip of the bluff behind my house. That natural stone patio with its built-in fireplace was the primary reason I had bought this house back in 1971. Sitting in a lawn chair on that patio, one had a sweeping view of Anchorage, and of Cook Inlet from the smoking cone of Mount Augustine in the south to Mounts McKinley and Forester to the north, and of the low mass of Mount Susitna, the Sleeping Lady, directly across the Inlet. Since all sunsets, regardless of the season, took place within this framework, I felt that I owned a treasure beyond value.

McGann must have read something in the tone and shortness of my reply. He did not broach the subject of Liz again.

"What have you got against doorbells, Ben? I remember you disconnected the one at your old Eagle River house, too."

"I guess I just found doorbells, chimes, or whatever, too impersonal. The bell dings, you don't know if it's a Girl Scout selling cookies, a cop, or some salesman. Now, with a real human knocking on your door, you can sometimes get a read on your visitor."

I opened the beers with a rusty opener hanging down beside the chimney on a thong, handed him one.

"A tentative tap-tap that's not repeated probably means a shy salesperson or religious solicitor who really hopes you don't answer. A light but firm knock, repeated once, may be your Girl Scout. A firm thump-thump repeated right away is an impatient cop. Bam-bam-bam with the flat of a hand means you've really pissed someone off and you might want to leave by the back door."

"Well I'll be damn! You've made a real science out of this door-knocking thing. Maybe you should write a book."

The sun was just beginning to slant down toward the Alaska Range, although it would be hours yet before it buried itself in the red and gold clouds that were building to the north.

"Enjoy the view, Jim—it's the most valuable thing I have left, right now. When we've half-killed our beer, you can tell me what kind of misery you've come to inflict on me."

McGann took me at my word, and we absorbed the view in silent appreciation for the next ten minutes.

"Ben, I want you to take another contract job for the CIC."

"Jim, you're full of it. If it's anything like the last job I took with you guys, the pay had better be one helluva lot better. I'm tired of getting shot at, and I really hate getting hit." I fingered the still-tender gouge in my left rib cage where a rifle bullet had punched through two summers ago.

McGann finished his beer in two hefty swallows and strode back to the house like a man with a mission. He returned with a pair of fresh brews, opened them, and sat down, a serious expression taking over his usually good-natured features.

"The Cold War was pretty intense during the 50's—you know because you were working with Operation Washtub at the time. It was a time when we had just begun to realize the extent of Soviet penetration of our society and our government agencies. We were finding Soviet moles in our CIA and in the various atomic weapons development agencies, agents that had been here for years or decades, working their way into positions of knowledge and responsibility. There was a steady clandestine flow of technical and policy information to the Soviet regime."

He looked over to see if he had my attention—the answer was, just barely.

"You probably heard of the World War Two Lend-Lease program? We had a steady stream of aircraft and war material flowing from the lower 48 through Canada and Alaska to Russia.

The big take-off point was at Great Falls, Montana."

I pretended disinterest, but it was obvious that the conversation was about to center on the red-starred C-47 I had reported to the FAA.

"Planes and cargo were assembled there and officially transferred to Russian ownership. American ferry pilots flew them to Ladd Field, and Russian crews took them on to Nome and across to Siberia. The official US policy was, 'Whatever the Russkies want, give it to 'em.' The Russians even sent 'procurement agents' to search our nation for their needs, and nobody paid much attention to what they hauled back to Russia."

By now, I was getting bored. I had been vaguely familiar with the program, and knew it was a giveaway program called "Lend-Lease" to make it easier for the taxpayers to swallow. Jim went on.

"A total of almost 8000 aircraft were flown from Great Falls to Ladd Field in Fairbanks, and on to Nome, over Siberia, and on to the European battle zone. Of these, about 700 were cargo planes, and all were stuffed with newly acquired cargo, both legitimate and otherwise. Soviet pilots and aircrew were ferried back to Great Falls in other cargo planes which, in turn, were loaded with more loot and dispatched to Russia."

"Jim, I know about the Lend-Lease, and I realize that the C-47 I found was probably one that had been given to the Russians, and probably went down in bad weather. But we don't know if it was flying full or on a back-haul."

He waved me silent.

"Just listen, dammit! In the process of all this confusion, sleeper agents by the dozens arrived, undocumented, stepped off the planes in civilian clothes and disappeared into the countryside. I'm going to lend you a book to read. It was written in 1952 by one of our officers who picked up on the stuff the Soviets were pulling off, and who tried to blow the whistle on them."

He handed me a small volume entitled, *From Major Jordan's Diaries*. A few Russia sympathizers and some stupid bureaucrats high in the system blocked and discredited him, so he eventually wrote a book which specifically documented the people places, and events in question.

"When you've read this, you'll understand enough that I can

explain the job I want you to take on. Then I'll come back and help you finish the six-pack."

McGann abruptly stood, ambled back to his car, and disappeared.

CHAPTER 11

Major Jordan's Diaries

I spent the evening and part of the next day reading the book that McGann had left me. Even had it not been connected with a possible job, I'd have found it interesting.

Major George Racey Jordan was an Air Corps officer assigned to the Lend-Lease program at the military air field at Great Falls, Montana. His job was to help expedite the transfer of airplanes and other war material to Russian authorities, who would load and send the planes off to Ladd Field and Nome, Alaska, thence to Russia via Siberia.

Early on, he noted unaccounted-for personnel arriving and departing as described by McGann. Jordan eventually began recording unusual and bizarre events in his diary, and documenting the dates, the cargo manifests, and the names of Russians involved. Later, before even a hint of the existence of an atom bomb had released, he noted two outbound shipments of uranium compounds and heavy water in the lend-lease C-47's. A part of almost every cargo consisted of dozens of cheap black suitcases which were always under armed guard and were uninspected, claimed to have "diplomatic immunity".

On several occasions, Jordan brought his own armed guards and forced the inspection of these suitcases. They contained stacks of technical manuals, library books covering scientific and technical subject, maps, plans and blueprints of manufacturing facilities, and US Government progress reports on various war and defense projects. Many had the top and bottom margins trimmed, as though to rid the documents of security classification markings.

Major Jordan tried to call the attention of his superiors to the shady goings on, but any subsequent investigations were quickly blocked at high levels. His writings detailed these and many more not-so-subtle intelligence and material gathering activities that Russian procurement personnel pulled off.

Jordan worked directly with the Russian colonel in charge of "procurement", and on many occasions objected to the export of classified information and equipment, and of critical (to our own war effort) war materials. The colonel would casually dial the number of a high-ranking US government official and hand Jordan the phone. The message he usually received was, "Give 'em what they want and quit making waves."

Finally, in the winter of 1944, Jordan contacted an Army Counter Intelligence Corps agent. The agent compiled a report based on Jordan's information and forwarded it through his own channels, recommending a follow-up. A meeting of concerned agencies took place in July; the records of the meeting have somehow not been located, and any proposed actions were seemingly ignored by higher authority.

McGann showed up at my bell-less front door the afternoon I finished Major Jordan's book. He gave the "police officer" knock, so I let him cool his heels on the front stoop before letting him in.

"I see you're carrying a six-pack. Come on around and we'll sit on the bluff and see if the bottle opener still works."

After testing the opener, we sat and admired the horizon for a while. When the beer was about half gone, McGann turned to me.

"What did you think of Jordan's journal?"

"Interesting and believable, especially after all that business with Alger Hiss, the Greenbergs, and with the moles turning up in the Atomic Energy Commission a few years back. What's it got to do with me?"

"The Russians seemed to get nervous after Jordan's report to the CIC agent. They became more discreet, but continued grabbing sensitive information and smuggling in undocumented personnel. They hastily gathered up a special small cargo load in a C-47 and sent it off toward Nome. The guy in charge was in a Russian colonel's uniform and had a briefcase cuffed to his wrist."

"Sounds like they were getting nervous," I said. "Starting to get high-value or very sensitive stuff out to Moscow before we got wise and cracked down on their operation."

"You've got it. And later bits of intel led us to believe that the briefcase carried by that colonel might be worth its weight in gold to us. We would have loved to get our hands on it, but..."

"Don't tell me—let me guess. The plane was lost on route to Siberia."

"Actually, the plane disappeared into bad weather after departing Great Falls for Fairbanks. Although we combed the countryside for a year afterward, nothing was ever found; it was assumed that it either went down over water somewhere, or crashed and burned. Then you routinely reported the recent location of a C-47 wreck, complete with the correct tail number and Russian star insignia."

"I didn't really want to report it, Jim. But I figured that, if there was ever a dispute against any salvage rights that I might want to claim, the official report would establish the date of my discovery."

"Ben, we've had that plane's tail number on our hot sheet for three decades, hoping that, by some miracle it might have crashed intact. The information in that briefcase is still of immense value to us. I can't tell you why now, but I will if you can recover it. How'n hell did you find that wreck anyway?"

I described to McGann how I had learned about the possible location of the C-47, and how I had found it. He shook his head in disbelief.

"So only Allison, you, and Buckner know about it? Keep it that way, Ben, for your own safety. Every Russian agent in the state has been watching for a sign of that C-47, and for the same reason we have. I've told the FAA to stay mum on the information you reported, but Soviet agents can be anywhere—there's even a possibility they have a mole or two inside the FAA."

"Jim, let's say this briefcase was of great value to us back in '44, why would it still be in 1974? That's several decades and several wars ago. And assuming I am dumb enough to take this job, what would you expect and how would get it done?"

"Ben, it would still be of great value. I can't tell you why now, but if it could be retrieved, you'd probably figure that out for yourself. The big problem—keeping it out of our hands would be of as much value to Russia as getting it would be to us. If they get wind of the possibility that we've found the wreck, they'll make a serious try for it. You could get caught in the middle."

CHAPTER 12

Curtains?

Jim shucked another bottle out of the beer carton and popped it open.

"The biggest problem is not letting the other side know that we have a lead on the location of the wreck. The Reds have an extensive network of agents in Alaska. It's so easy to move back and forth between here and Siberia that they keep inserting fresh people when we get too close to any of their agents. That means we can't just mount up a salvage expedition with a couple of Chinook helicopters and go jerk it out of there. In the first place, it may not jerk so easily. In the second place, any kind of unusual activity like that, they'd be on it like a duck on a junebug. And believe me, if the item still exists, it's of such importance to them that they'd use whatever force they can get away with."

"You're not exactly selling me on this job, McGann. You don't want to fight 'em with a task force, but you're willing for me to go in alone. I don't think so."

"What I want you to do, Hunnicutt, is go back to the crash site, get inside the airplane, and see if the briefcase survived. If it did, get it back to me."

"Why did you pick me? You have the entire US Army Alaska to pick from, and you wouldn't have to pay them any more than soldier pay. And I'll tell you right now— if I go, I won't be cheap labor."

"We don't want to stir things up, Ben. If you go back in as an individual, with no publicity, it'll hardly be noticed. We can't set up any kind of expedition without it being leaked, maybe even making the news. If the Russians even suspect we have the item, they'll change certain systems and make things tougher for us."

"Let me think it over, Jim. There'll be conditions, and you probably won't like them, but I've got to go over this in my mind and come up with a minimum risk plan. Just getting inside that wreck will be a major problem."

I described the location and harrowing conditions surrounding the wreck to Jim, and made it a point to emphasize that it was not a one-man job.

"If I take the job, I'm gonna ask Mike Gearhart to go in with me; I trust him to keep quiet about it, and he's good with the kind of field expedients we'll have to use to either break in, or get it down. He had my back on your warhead theft affair and handled it well. Your outfit will take care of any expenses, just like last time. Right?"

"OK," said McGann, after some thought. "Handle it your way, but keep it quiet. And let me know shortly. The more time wasted, the more likely the other side will find out and take counter measures."

I drove to Eagle River the next morning, intending to present the matter to Mike Gearhart and see if he was interested. I had a good idea that the job would appeal to him; Mike was a hunting and fishing guide, at home in the back country. He was also somewhat of a soldier of fortune, taking on hairy situations like this just for the excitement.

When I arrived at his neat log cabin high on the north wall of Eagle River Valley, I stopped my Ford pickup dead in the middle of the road and stared.

There were brightly colored curtains in the windows, several blooming hanging baskets on the wide front porch, and a clothes line festooned with female attire stretched out in the side yard. Could Mike have moved without telling me? It didn't seem likely, but his allowing his rustic home place to become so blatantly feminized was even less likely.

I pulled into his drive, got out, and went up to knock on the front door. This was the first time I had gotten that far without being intercepted, usually by Mike hefting a shotgun. His was the last dwelling on the road, and he suspected anyone who came that far of planning some sort of mischief.

Mike, an ex-air force captain, had for a short while worked with me on the Washtub operation of the 1950's. He found Alaska to his liking, and had claimed it as his own. Mike became a hunting guide—a good one, I was told—and used the income from that trade to finance his own adventuring throughout the territory. He was a loner by nature, and held in contempt anyone who wasn't comfortable in the mountains or on the rivers of his wild domain. We had hunted together—hunted man, to be truthful—and had established the bond that can only come from that brutal experience.

I knew from my last visit to his cabin, a drinking bout that had got me in trouble with Liz, that he had fallen for a lady he had met in a gun shop. It seemed that they were compatible, equally stubborn, and independent, and had spent significant time rolling around on the grizzly-skin rug beside his fireplace.

I had not yet met Neeta, but had fully expected them to have an early clash regarding who would change to suit whom. Seeing the new frippery decorating his cabin, I braced myself to encounter what must be a dominant female, probably capable of whipping me in a fair fight. Mike was a six-foot-six lanky counterpart of Gary Cooper, and it would take some sort of lady bulldog to tame him.

CHAPTER 13

Neeta

I hesitantly advanced to the front door and knocked (Mike didn't believe in doorbells either). The door opened and I faced a child, or maybe a teenager. Through the screen door, I couldn't make out her features or expression, just that she was standing patiently, waiting for me to say something.

"Is Mike around?" I asked.

The voice that answered was not that of a child.

"Oh, sure. He's out back working on my truck. Come on through."

She opened the screen and ushered me inside. I could now see that I was talking with a small woman, probably a bit over five feet tall with straw-colored hair and a smooth browned complexion that told of many hours outdoors. Her age, probably early 30's; her figure, if described by an interested male, would be called "perky". She was wearing a skirt and sweater, the latter putting the "perk" in perky. Except for her eyes, which hinted at a wisdom which only came from hard knocks, she could have been a college co-ed or a first-grade teacher.

"I'm Neeta," she said, extending her hand. I took it and introduced myself.

"I'm Ben Hunnicutt."

"Oh, yes—Mike's told me about you, and about the scrapes you two have gotten into. I'll go get him; he'll want you to sit for a cup of coffee and a chat, I'm sure."

She seated me at the small table by the front window and

went out the back door.

This delicate little lady and Mike! I tried to wrap my mind around a vision of the pair together—then imagining that pair alongside of Red Buckner and his six-foot wife, I almost laughed out loud.

Mike had told me of Neeta fending off a sexual assault in her Trapper Creek cabin, splintering a rifle stock across the attacker's face and sending him looking for medical aid. And he had said her choice of hunting rifles was a Winchester 338 Magnum. Since then, I had always pictured her as a big strong woman, tough as the country in which she had chosen to live.

The back door opened and Neeta returned, followed by Mike Gearhart in mechanic's coveralls. We shook hands, Mike shucked the coveralls, and we sat down by the front window. Neeta joined us, bringing cups and the coffee pot, filling the cups, and offering the fixings.

I fingered the colorful curtains framing the window and gave Mike a small grin.

"About time you brightened this place up a bit, Mike. But I didn't know you hired a built-in decorator for the job. What does the bear think about all that?"

Both Mike and Neeta blushed a bit, and Neeta replied.

"That bear hasn't had it so good since he left his berry bushes. We take very good care of him, don't we Mike?"

"That we do, Honey; that we do." He turned to me.

"Sorry we haven't bumped into each other lately, Ben. What with Neeta deciding to spend some time here, I've been a little busy redoing the place. Right now, I'm building a step under the driver's door of her truck so she can step up and get in easier. If it works out, I may do the same to mine."

"I been telling you for years, Mike, that big 250 of yours is more truck than you need, and a gas hog to boot."

"Well," he came back, "you just try pulling a 26-foot cabin cruiser behind that little half-ton Ford of yours. I'll come along behind you to clear away the wreckage."

Having gotten the required insults out of the way, we each turned our attention to the coffee, then to the reason for my visit.

I first cautioned Mike and Neeta concerning the need for secrecy, after which I went over the events leading to the discovery of the plane wreck, and to the unexpected military and political factors now at play.

"Now as to the actual job of getting into the airplane," I began, "I don't think there's any hope of getting it un-wedged and down to the ground without a lot of equipment and a lot of luck. And somebody would damn sure get hurt.

"To me, the best bet is to rig a way to safely get up to the main body and somehow cut an entryway. I figure it'll need three good men. If you're interested, I figure you for one—you're ex-Air Force, you know planes, and you're mechanically sharp. I've arranged for you to be paid the same as for that warhead recovery operation back in 1970. If you know anyone else that might be qualified, and is trustworthy, I'll check him out. If not, I'll sound out Mike Lineman, down on the Kenai. Of course," I grinned at him, "two Mikes on the same job might sink the whole operation."

"Just a darn minute!" came a sharp voice from the third chair at the table. "You've got number three sitting right beside you, and you're talking around me like I'm not here. I've ridden out three winters in a cabin at Trapper Creek, and I've fought off bears, moose, and one two-legged asshole. 'Cause I'm small doesn't mean I'm not able."

Mike and I looked at each other, I with a questioning expression, he with the resigned look of a man holding a pair of deuces when the dealer stands pat.

"Ben," he said, "I think she could handle it OK. Never yet heard her complain. And," he added with a smile, "if I said otherwise, I'd be a dead man."

"I'm not really that bad," she said to me with a straight face. "He just doesn't know me well enough yet to take chances. You don't either, so be careful!"

We returned to the subject, and I sketched out the C-47 and its precarious position above the gorge. We kicked around various approaches to the problem, pretty well settling on the opinion that the only feasible course was to get up on the remainder of the right wing and use it as a working platform to breach the fuselage.

I stressed the fact that the primary mission was to obtain the briefcase, if it still existed, and to secretly secure it before moving forward with any salvage work. It was also very important, according to McGann, that the other side not know we had it. If the Russians knew, they would take countermeasures which might largely reduce the value of our find.

I still didn't know exactly what the briefcase might hold, but I was getting an idea. If I was right, I might soon wish someone else had discovered the wreck.

Mike's first comment was to the effect that we'd need a lot of rope for safety if we were going to be climbing around on an aluminum wing with a rounded surface which might be wet or slippery with lichen or moss. After a few more minutes of study, Neeta suggested we acquire a few lengths of rope ladder of the type used for emergency fire escapes in dwellings.

"That'd save having to climb the side wall of the gorge every time we want to access or leave the wing stub," she explained. "It's going to take a lot of going and coming to get tools and gear into position to actually make an entry."

Mike nodded in agreement; I felt that maybe Neeta had paid her way already.

We talked and planned into the evening, and by the time I felt I should go, everyone seemed caught up in enthusiasm for the expedition. According to McGann, time was precious if we wanted to get in and out again before some inkling of our mission reached unfriendly ears. We agreed to use tomorrow for gathering gear and supplies, and to alert Red Buckner for the short-notice charter. We hoped to be on the way the morning after.

CHAPTER 14

The Potential for Disaster

I hadn't been home an hour when Jim McGann called and asked if I had my crew, and, if so, when we planned to leave for the crash site. I brought him up to date, also telling him who my crew was going to be, and immediately had to dodge a cloud of flak for taking a woman along. After five minutes of telling him why I had chosen Neeta, and emphasizing that I wasn't about to change my mind, Jim gave in. He did tell me to waste no time; things were warming up.

"I got calls from DC telling me that the Russians somehow got wind that something was up. Their Ambassador is asking questions about the rumor of a Russian plane found in Alaska, and has been in contact with a person here that we know to be one of their agents."

"Dammit, McGann, can't you keep them off our necks until we have a chance to at least look for the briefcase? An item that small can be hard to find in a wrecked cargo plane that's been in place for 30 years."

"I can't do much to slow them down," he said, "but I'm starting to put together a back-up team to throw in if things get too hairy. It'll take a day or two. I sure wish we could have some means of direct communication with you while you're at the site. Our radios won't reach that far with the mountains in the way."

"No way to set up a relay system?"

"Not on this short a notice. Remember, it's imperative that you get in and get out without their knowing you found the item.

If they send in some people while you're working, it'll be hard to get it by them without some degree of force. And if they know you have it, they can eventually nullify its usefulness to us."

"An awful lot of fuss over something that you refuse to describe to me, Jim."

"Just look for some books or documents in a briefcase, cuffed to somebody's wrist. You'll understand afterward. Call me right before you take off so I'll know the operation has started. I'm gonna try and arrange a back-up in case you get in a tight spot."

We spent the following day collecting gear and shopping for any we didn't have. I had a bunch of Air Force "In Flight" rations, which were very similar to Army C-Rations. I much preferred them to MRE's or Lurps. Mike disappeared onto Elmendorf Air Force Base to look up some old buddies and pick their brains on the subject of aircraft rescue and salvage. On his return, he had a case of fresh MRE's and a strange looking hand axe. I hefted the axe; it was a bit heavier than a commercial tool of like dimensions, had a cutting blade and sharp pick point, like a mountaineer's ice axe, and had a hooked device on the handle-end that resembled a super-sized old fashioned can opener—but much larger and sturdier. I asked the tool's purpose, and Mike just grinned. His only comment:

"That's how we get inside if nothing else works."

Recalling McGann's concern about Russian competition in taking possession of the airplane, I insisted that all three of us bring our hunting rifles and a bit more than the usual amount of ammunition. If the Soviets wanted to turn this expedition into World War Three, I had no intention of dying for lack of shooting back.

We met the next morning at Lake Hood with a truckload of equipment and camping supplies. Red had a Cessna floatplane waiting, emptied out and ready for us and our gear. We pretty well used up all the space in the plane and were climbing into our seats when Jim McGann came trotting up, out of breath and panting. We left our seats and I introduced him to Neeta and Red. He shook hands with all, a curious expression on his face when he had to reach down for Neeta and Red.

"With luck," he said to me, "you'll be there and back before the other side gets their stuff straight. And with the item, I hope."

"Well", I said, "today being Sunday, and a lot of recreational planes using the lake, we'll probably go unnoticed as we leave." He glanced at the lake, liberally sprinkled with light aircraft aligning themselves for takeoff to the various fishing grounds or the wilderness cabins that so appeal to Alaskans.

"Hope you're right. It'll simplify matters if the Russians don't involve themselves in this mess, but I think they'll try if they think there's a chance of success."

"Remember the priorities, Ben. First priority is to get the briefcase without anyone knowing. Second, get it even if they'll know you have it. Third, get you and your crew back in one piece. Good luck." He shook hands all around and, in his loose-jointed way, meandered back toward his car. When it dawned on me that saving our skins was his third priority, I turned to shout a few words at him, but he was gone.

I turned to Red.

"Sorry about all that mysterious stuff that Jim was saying. He evidently thinks I told you all about the problems we might have—and I probably should've. Let's just say we may have competition while going after this wreck. It shouldn't involve you once we're dropped off. Just wait for Jim's call to pick us up. We have about a week's groceries, so pick us up a week from today if you haven't heard from him. OK?"

"Ben, I personally think this whole deal has the potential for disaster. Too disorganized, too shoot-from-the hip, not enough prior planning—but hell, it's your asses. Let's do it!"

CHAPTER 15

The Old Lady with the Red Stars

Red put his heavily loaded floatplane down in the shallow lake and beached it at my old camp site. I checked the area for signs of later visitors, but found only a few bear tracks and a fresh pile of droppings. Having expressed his opinion of us, the bear had apparently wandered off up the Gerstle River valley in search of its next meal.

The four of us soon had the plane emptied of gear and supplies and Red, after a petunia break in the brush, climbed into the pilot's seat and signaled us to push him off from shore. As the plane drifted away, he leaned out and called back,

"A week from today if not told otherwise."

I circled thumb and forefinger in the 'Okay' sign, and he fired up the engine, swung into the wind, and launched himself toward Anchorage.

We set up camp and arranged a shelter tarp for the tools and supplies. Recalling the fresh bear sign (not my earlier black bear visitor but a fair-sized grizzly, from the looks of the tracks), we put the food in a sack and hung it high in a nearby tree. Neeta turned out to be an adept climber and, as I watched her do more than her share of the work without help or instructions, it became obvious that she was a worthwhile addition to our team.

By default, I had inherited command of our little party, primarily because I was the only person who knew the situation and the terrain. I waved them over to the sitting log.

"We've plenty of daylight left. I'll walk you all in to the wreck site so you can see what we're up against. Everybody armed at all times, chambers empty. There are both grizzly and black bear here. And sooner or later, there may be unwelcome people."

We stood under the suspended C-47, staring upward in mute fascination and puzzling over the challenge of gaining access and entry to the forbidding metal cylinder that was formerly the willing servant of those who flew her.

"Tomorrow, I'll climb up to the right wing and rig a rope ladder for you guys to use. Probably rig a safety line along the wing while I'm up there."

We peered at Neeta in surprise. In about five seconds she had devised what seemed the only feasible and safe way to get us up to where we could work on gaining entry.

She continued, "Or you can throw a rope over the wing from here, weighted with a hammer or something. Tie me to one end and the two of you grab the other and haul me up. If I can get to that aileron that's hanging loose, I can tie the ladder to its hinge. That ought to hold you OK."

In another five seconds, she had figured a better alternate scheme. Mike and I looked at each other and shook our heads in wonderment. She caught the look and her face fell.

"I'm sorry—maybe it's a dumb idea. I was trying to be helpful, and it's the first thing that occurred to me."

"It's a great idea." I said, giving her diminutive frame a delicate hug. "Mike or I would probably have thought of it in another day or two."

We returned to camp in silence, each probably mulling over tomorrow's rigging chore and wondering what would go wrong.

We made camp, I unfolding a newly-purchased mountain tent with an outside frame, overly mechanical in my opinion, but fast to erect and take down. Mike and Neeta shook out an old fashioned two-person shelter, putting it up a respectful distance from mine, for which I was silently thankful. I didn't need any more reminders that Liz was no longer around to help warm my tent.

Since we might be here for the entire week, we dug a military style latrine trench well down wind, clearing away all the nearby vegetation except that screening it from camp. Nobody wanted an unexpected encounter with a prowling bear while in such an extremely vulnerable position. I left three forked sticks driven into the ground in a convenient location, one for the small entrenching shovel I left propped against it, one for a roll of toilet paper protected from the elements by a number ten coffee can, and one for the rifle that would surely accompany each user.

By the time daylight had started to fade, our bivouac was finished and we had gravitated to the sitting log and the fire before it.

"Damn nice to fly in on a decent sized airplane," I remarked. "We didn't have to worry too much about the weight of our gear and tools, and whether we could haul it all on our backs."

"I second that!" said Mike. "It would have been a shame to have to leave this behind." He reached into a stuff-bag and produced a bottle of fair-to-middling scotch.

"I didn't bring the really good stuff, but I 'spect this'll taste just fine after a day of climbing around on that airplane."

Without comment, Neeta and I dug out our cups and watched as Mike carefully poured three fingers in each. I raised mine in salute.

"To the old lady with the red stars—may she welcome us aboard."

We hoisted our cups in the direction of the gorge and drank to the ancient C-47 and to the job ahead.

CHAPTER 16

A Slippery Slope

Despite the tiring activities of the previous day, we were up early Monday morning thinking of the puzzles and problems confronting us. After a good breakfast which used up most of the dozen eggs, we had brought with us, we dug out a coil of light rope, a rope ladder, and a few hand tools. Hauling them and our rifles up the gorge to the wreck limbered us up and had us anticipating the challenge ahead.

We immediately embarked on Neeta's plan. After several attempts, a thrown rope weighted with Mike's odd-ball axe sailed over the right wing of the C-47 and thunked into the stream bed on the opposite side. We fashioned one end into a sling loop into which Neeta could sit and secured the coiled ladder across her thighs. Mike and I took our place at the dangling end of the rope, knotted it for a good grip, and began to pull.

Even as light as Neeta was, the lift took all our weight and strength. The friction generated by the rope being pulled across the broad surface of the wing stub and over the edges created tremendous resistance to our effort—had our load been anyone larger or heavier, the attempt would have failed.

Eventually, after much grunting and groaning, Neeta found herself face to face with the aileron, which dangled at an angle from the trailing edge of the wing. We stopped hauling and waited while she freed the top of the rope ladder and attached it to the aileron. We had tied mountaineering-style carabiners to each vertical rope, so all she had to do was pass each through the gap between the wing and the aileron, loop it back, and snap it over the rope.

When we began hauling again, Neeta was able to pull herself up onto the wing surface, pushing the ladder ahead and unrolling it as she went. The rope by which we had hoisted her to the wing went slack in our hands.

"Neeta," Mike shouted, "Keep a good grip on that ladder. It's the only safety line you have now."

She reached the leading edge of the wing and rolled the ladder off the edge. Its bottom cross rung stopped about a foot from the ground, swinging loosely back and forth in a manner that was far from reassuring. Mike and I searched the stony stream bed for two of the heaviest rocks we could lift together and manhandled them over to the foot of the ladder. We cut some excess length from the rope we had used to lift Neeta to the wing, tying the bottom of the ladder to the rock anchors. The rope ladder now seemed taut and steady enough that a climber wouldn't swing like a human pendulum.

I decided to act as test pilot, Mike standing at the ready in case the ladder needed steadying as I climbed. The climb revealed no unexpected difficulties once I had adjusted to the natural springiness of the rope uprights. When I looked over the top of the wing, I saw Neeta sprawled at the outer end of the wing where it had broken away just outboard of the engine. She was tying a length of her hoisting rope to a section of spar protruding from the mass of dirt and aluminum where the wing stub had ground its way into the valley wall. On seeing me, she grinned and scrunched her way backwards, paying out the rope as she came.

"I didn't see anything to tie to at the cabin-end of the wing," she said, "but we should be able to break out a couple of adjacent windows and loop the rope in one and out the other, and tie it off. This wing is slippery with some kinda moss or algae that's grown through the years. We'll need this safety line to tie to, or hold on to."

Neeta was right, as usual. The dust, dirt, and debris that had settled on the aluminum surfaces over three decades of exposure had furnished a bed for a thin skin of various green-tinged mosses that apparently soaked up moisture. Under the hand, the surface felt like a thin coating of slippery mud. It would be treacherous to walk or to crawl on, as the airplane had lodged in a slightly nose-down attitude and the wing surface slanted forward and downward.

As I pulled myself up onto the wing by the ladder rungs, I could feel the ladder stretch as Mike began to ascend.

"Have you got the axe?" I asked over my shoulder.

"Yep," he replied, reaching up and putting it in my hand.

I very carefully crawled over toward the fuselage, slipping forward on the wing despite determined efforts not to do so. When Neeta saw that I was having problems, she passed the end of the safety rope through the aileron gap and threw it to me. 'At least,' I thought, as I looped it around my arm, 'if I slide off, I'll be stopped before I hit the ground.'

I continued to crawl toward the fuselage, Neeta staying in place anchored to the rope ladder stretched across the wing, and Mike watching from the top of the ladder at the front of the wing. A few feet from the main body of the aircraft, the wing's surface evolved into a smooth concave fillet which rounded up and blended with the vertical skin of the body. There was no traversing that section without losing traction and sliding forward and off the wing. I remained immobile for several minutes, trying to come up with an idea that would get me close enough to the side of the body of the plane to somehow anchor the rope's end. Without some kind of safety line, we were unlikely to force an entry without at least one of us slipping and falling to the rocky ground 30 feet below.

"Mike," Neeta called, "get your rifle and shoot out the center window. If Ben can stretch far enough to grab the edge of the hole, he can hang on and use the axe to knock out the next window and tie the rope through. Better bring a pair of gloves too."

While Mike was retrieving his rifle and digging through his pack for the gloves, I weighed the wisdom of her solution. Mike did not—he had instantly obeyed, ready to accept Neeta as a voice of authority. I was oddly happy to realize this, and had a feeling that they would become a nicely matched couple in temperament, if not in appearance.

"Mike," I called, "try to get an angle that puts the bullet through the window and up through the top of the plane. The slanting shot will make a bigger hole, and if the damn plane is loaded with dynamite, you might miss it."

Mike's head and the barrel of his rifle were just showing over the front edge of the wing as I spoke. I saw his eyes widen.

"Damn, Ben. I never thought about what might be inside. Do you think we should try it?"

"Heck, hand me the rifle. I can maybe hold it at arm's length and get the angle I need."

"No way, Ben. The kick of that Weatherby Magnum will send you scooting over the edge sure as hell and I don't want my rifle and scope all busted up."

"OK, you do it from there then. If you shoot that Plexiglas at as shallow an angle as possible and still penetrate it, I doubt that the bullet will do anything more than punch another hole in the roof and just keep on going. Whatever cargo was in that hull is probable scattered all up and down the deck, not stacked window high."

Mike shook his head doubtfully and shot a questioning glance at Neeta.

"He's right, Mike. Get on with it."

He shifted around at the top of the ladder, braced, and re-braced himself.

"OK', I heard, "Watch your face and eyes. I shoot in five seconds."

I turned my face away and awaited the shot.

CHAPTER 17

The Ultimate Can Opener

There was a wicked crack as Mike's Weatherby launched a bullet near my head at well over 3,000 feet per second, the entire airplane resonating to the shock and sound. I had my hands over my ears and my face turned down, one of my smarter moves that day. Particles of Plexiglas and aluminum stung my exposed neck and head, but none drew blood.

There were seven windows on the right side of the fuselage, all rectangular and about 15 inches wide and a foot high. The plastic panes were dirty and begrimed from dust and blowing sand—nothing could be seen of the interior. The one Mike had shot now had a small section blown out at the top. The center was crazed and cracked, but still clung together.

I very cautiously came to a crouch, the safety rope still in a half-hitch around my left arm. With the axe in my right hand, I lunged forward and upward, burying the sharp pick point in the broken window and desperately grasping the handle. With the lunge, my feet had gone from under me and I sprawled over the wing root, held in place only by my grip on the axe handle and its point penetrating the window. I pulled myself up close to the window, used my gloved left hand to punch away the loose shards of plastic, and shoved the hand through. Anchored then by my left hand, I worked the pick-head out of the window and used it to chop through the next window forward, clearing nearly all the fragments from the frame, and hooking the axe head inside.

While I was standing in that awkward position trying to figure what to do next, I felt the rope around my left arm tighten. Neeta was working her way along the safety rope, finally reaching me and freeing the rope end. She pushed her slender arm into the aft window and fed the end inside until there was enough to whip back and forth until I could grasp it through the forward window with my right hand. I withdrew my hand, clutching the rope and leaving the axe hanging in the aperture. After the simple act of knotting the rope into a tight loop, we finally had a safety line to secure ourselves while we did whatever was needed to attain entry.

All of our exertion had resulted in a relatively simple work area: 20 feet of wing with a taut safety rope stretching over its length, and a rope ladder secured across the wing and anchored to the ground 30 feet below by two heavy stones. We could travel the length of the wing moving hand-over-hand along the safety rope. And we could secure ourselves to it with a loose loop of shorter rope if the task at hand seemed to warrant such.

I peered through the shot-out window in an attempt to determine the condition of the interior and the cargo, whatever it may have been. The row of grimy windows on each side of the aircraft admitted little light. I could see that the cargo, however it had been tied down, was now a jumble of loose containers scattered about the interior, most jammed forward and blocking the way to the navigator's compartment and cockpit. No real detail was visible in the semi-darkness of the interior.

"How about we break for lunch?" I asked, my gut reminding me that we had taken most of the morning setting things up for our grand entry into the Red Starred Lady. Mike readily agreed, Neeta not so readily; I could see that she was burning with curiosity and could hardly wait to get inside the C-47.

We climbed awkwardly down the springy rope ladder, recovered our rifles, and trudged back to camp discussing the next stage of our project. As we sat on our log munching away at our various midday snacks (mine, two nourishing Baby Ruth candy bars and a reheated cup of instant coffee), Neeta and I kicked around ideas for breaking into the body of the plane.

"There's an escape hatch above the pilot's seat," I offered, "but I can't see anyone getting up on top of that rounded fuselage and crawling forward without sliding off and killing themselves. And I don't know if there's a workable outside lever or handle."

"I looked over the cockpit windows." said Neeta. "First, they're too small for even me to get through, and second, we can't get to them. We're just going to have to make a hole in the cargo section where we broke out the small windows."

I looked over at Mike, expecting an idea or opinion from him. To my surprise, instead of looking worried or thoughtful, he seemed smug and unconcerned.

"No thoughts on the subject, Mike?"

"No sweat, people," he said airily. "I'll get us in there."

Though we tried to worm more information from him, Mike just smiled to himself and kept mum. When he finished his snack, he found a soft spot in the grass, propped his jacket under his head, and took a nap.

Neeta and I, bursting with curiosity though we were, had little choice but to wait him out in silence, or to follow his example. The sun felt comforting after the damp shadowy shade of the gorge, so we chose our own nests and followed suit.

Gathered together on the wing of the plane, near the broken-out windows, we watched Mike as he examined the row of windows and the surrounding aluminum skin of the fuselage. I noticed that there were several areas of fading lettering stenciled: "CUT HERE FOR EMERGENCY RESCUE".

Mike explained, "These are areas that don't have any main structural members under the skin, so you can cut a hole and make an unblocked entry. You all better stand clear."

He removed the axe which was still hanging from the forward of the two windows we had broken out, and shifted his position to the rear, or uphill side of the safety rope. Using the point of the axe, he pricked four marks on the aluminum skin in a rectangular pattern which encompassed one of the "cut here" areas. Standing and braced by the taut safety rope, he swung the sharp pick hard against each of the four marks, leaving in each a hole resembling a 45-caliber bullet hole.

Neeta and I, on our knees and hanging on to the safety rope, looked at each other in puzzlement. Surely Mike wasn't planning on punching several hundred holes in the tough aluminum and trying to rip the section free along the dotted lines?

He reversed the axe and showed us the odd configuration at the end of the handle. It had seemed familiar to me when I first saw it, but didn't ring any bells. Now, the light dawned—the handle was configured like an old-fashioned manual can opener, the kind you jammed into a can and levered a stout cutting edge around the lid of a can one short cut at a time.

Mike grinned and plunged the cutter into one of the pre-punched top holes. He levered it an inch at a time across to the other top hole, exactly as one would while opening a can of beans. When the ragged cut was complete, he inserted the cutter into a bottom hole.

"This is called a crash axe," he explained. "It's issued to fire and rescue teams around airports. Takes a lot of effort to use, but it generally does the job."

He made the cut upward to the top hole, then withdrew the cutter and made another upward cut on the opposite side. With the point of the tool inserted at the top, he pulled the skin away from the frame. Motioning me to help, he grasped the top of the flap of aluminum and we pulled it outward and bent it down out of the way. There was one horizontal aluminum rod barring the way—a structural brace of some sort. Mike made short work of removing it with the blade of the crash axe. The resulting opening was barely large enough for Mike or me to scrape through, and was partly blocked by some sort of container.

CHAPTER 18

Earth to Earth

The three of us stared through the opening in the hull of the plane. Nothing was visible except dark shapes in the shadows beyond. Finally, Neeta dropped to her knees.

"I'll go in," she said. "I'm smaller than you guys. I can get by that black crate, or whatever it is. Maybe I can pull it away to make more room for you."

We helped her through the opening, guiding her clear of the jagged edges of the aluminum skin where Mike had used his super-can opener. She slipped inside.

"I'll be damned," we heard her say. "It's a suitcase. No, it's a whole mess of suitcases. Some have broken open and there're tons of books, magazines, and documents scattered all over the place. Looks like some metal drums and wood crates jammed up front. Here, I'll let you guys in."

The object that had blocked our entry disappeared and Neeta's face took its place.

"Come on in. Most of the mess is those suitcases—the heavy stuff is all jammed up front. Gonna' be a job getting through to the cockpit."

Having read Major Jordan's book, I pretty-well knew what to expect in the way of cargo. And he had described the 40 or 50 new black suitcases that would be filled with sensitive or classified documents and detailed maps, plans, and descriptions of American war plants. It was too dark in the cargo bay to read the scattered books and documents, but most would be valueless now, thirty years after their theft. I moved forward, shoving, and kicking black suitcases out of the way. About ten feet from the door to the radioman/navigator's cubical, the way was clogged with the heavier drums and crates which had flown forward when the plane came to its final stop.

"Mike, could you start trying to get this stuff out of the way while I go back and get the flashlights? Leave the real heavy items 'till I get back to help."

I returned shortly with the lights, grumbling at myself for having forgotten them in the first place. When I climbed back up onto the wing, Neeta was sitting just outside the entry hole going through old magazines.

"Hey, look. Here are some fashion magazines from 1944. Looks like the Russians were on the lookout for stuff for their ladies, too. I found one suitcase full of perfumes, toilet articles, and makeup compacts."

"Anything you want is yours," I responded. "Or rather, I should have said, anything that we can carry in the airplane."

The flashlight showed the interior of the cargo bay to be 25 or 30 feet long, and maybe six or seven feet wide, the heaviest items in a disorganized pile blocking the door forward. I entered the bay and made my way up to where Mike was grunting and struggling with some small metal barrels. Out of curiosity I examined several with a flashlight. One was marked, "Uranium Nitrate", the other had the content over-painted and a four-digit number hand-painted next to it. The black over-paint was thin and chalky with age—I was able to scrape it away with my pocket knife to reveal the original marking, "Uranium Oxide".

The metal drums were far too heavy to lift, even using our concerted effort.

"Mike," I said, "take particular note of any of these steel drums that might be leaking or broken open. I think there may be some radioactive stuff in them."

"They look OK so far," he replied. "But they're so damn heavy I can't move 'em out of the way."

I crawled over the various crates, boxes, and barrels looking for something we could use as a pry bar. Finally, near the cargo door on the left side, I was surprised to spot a real pry bar strapped to the rear bulkhead. It made sense that the people loading the plane would have to shift cargo while securing it for flight, or freeing it for unloading, and I appreciated their foresight. I went forward with the bar and, between the two of us, we managed to clear a way to the narrow door leading to the radioman/navigator/flight engineer's compartment.

Smaller items had found their way through the door and had blocked and cluttered the narrow aisle through the compartment which opened onto the flight deck. Mike and I cleared them out of the way, and I checked the small cubicle for signs of its previous tenant. What appeared to be a bundle of wool clothing was plastered against the forward bulkhead of the small cubical. Closer examination showed it to be the remnants of a Russian uniform shrouding the remains of its owner.

"The flight deck's gonna' be a real mess." I predicted. My expectations were realized as Mike and I stepped into the flight cabin and stood behind the pilot's and copilot's seats.

It appeared at first as though someone had discarded three sets of heavy woolen clothing, draping, and flattening them against the array of switches, gauges, levers, and controls that made up the forward wall of the cabin. They were not all neatly laid out; several were twisted into configurations foreign to the human anatomy.

Closer examination revealed that the uniforms, though not filled out, were occupied. The cloth was mottled in color, parts of it crumbling or nibbled away by small rodent teeth. A tentative tug at an arm showed it firmly stuck to whatever surface was beneath it. There were bones, cleanly picked bare by whatever insect or rodent life had lived in, or had found its way into the airplane. Some parchment-like skin remained—enough, combined with the clothing and some stiffened ligaments, to keep the bones in place. The skulls of the three bodies were clearly recognizable for what they were, though there was some fragmenting. The three comprised a flattened mass which seemed to have grown into the forward structure of the cockpit.

I heard a sudden intake of breath from Mike as he moved to a place behind my shoulder from which he could see the remains.

"I've heard the expression, 'Earth to earth, dust to dust'," he said, "and I'm beginning to understand it. Those guys are literally melting back into the earth. If they were outside, and if the animals couldn't get at them, they would have dissolved into the ground and become a part the earth again."

CHAPTER 19

Four Books

I heard Neeta working her way up behind us. I looked questioningly at Mike; he shrugged and remained silent.

"Neeta, there are remains of the crew up here. They're old, and it's not too bad, but you needn't see them if you don't want to. We can do anything that needs doing."

"I'll look." she said. She moved around us and took a long silent look at the crew. She then presented a very military salute, held it for a few seconds, and returned to the cargo bay.

"Well, I guess I'd better get what I came for, if it's still here."

I looked over the crewmen, finally settling on the one who had been wearing the most elaborate boots. His left hand was out of sight, shielded by the body of another. With some difficulty I moved the top body. It seemed glued to the floor. My efforts elicited crackling and tearing sounds as the stiffened, dried out body parts flexed for the first time in three decades. Wedging him out of the way with my right boot, I moved the left arm of the body of the presumed courier officer.

The same sounds issued from the disturbed limb, and a set of handcuffs added a metallic note. I could see the briefcase, apparently undamaged by the crash but mouse-gnawed and with tiny perforations left by worms or insect larvae. I hesitated to further mutilate the remains by tearing the bones and ligaments apart to free the cuffs, even though I knew it might be necessary.

Mike solved my dilemma; he grasped the leather handles of the briefcase with one hand, the body of the case with the other, and twisted. The brittle dried out leather cracked and broke, the briefcase coming free in a small cloud of dust and leather fragments. Mike handed it to me and I made my way back to our improvised entrance, and out onto the wing.

"Mike, I've got to look this over and find out if it's the thing we want. Then, I've got to hide it until we get out of here. I'm going back to camp. You and Neeta can explore all you want; if you find a ton of gold, save ten pounds for me."

I went to the ladder via the safety line, climbed down to the welcome earth below, slung my rifle, and headed to camp with the battered briefcase tucked under my arm.

I propped my back against the sitting log and laid the briefcase on the ground before me. It was an old-fashioned briefcase with an expandable accordion pleated bottom. A strap over the mouth of the case, secured by a brass snap lock on one end, effectively blocked access. I hadn't the stomach to go back and search the courier officer for the key, so I grasped the stitched end and gave a hard twist. The rotted threads gave up without a struggle and the mouth of the case yawned open.

Aside from some spider webs and a few brittle cocoons and insect carcasses, the case contained one tightly wrapped package and a holstered pistol—a Tokarev Model TT33. It was a familiar enemy to me; a similar weapon in the hand of a Chinese officer had punched several holes in my tender hide during the Korean "Police Action" in 1953. That officer had died valiantly under fire, an American 45 automatic punching a much larger hole that the 30 caliber Tokarev.

I pulled the Russian-made pistol from its crumbling leather flap holster and eased the slide back. The black plastic grips with a large star embossed near the top were clean and functional. The gun was still loaded and a round was in the chamber. Whether or not it would operate properly was debatable; the action was stiff, the arm coated with rust, and the magazine rusted tightly into the grip. But these Russian designed small arms had a reputation for being just as reliable as US issue arms, and I wouldn't bet against this old warrior doing its job if there was need.

The package was wrapped in something resembling oilcloth and sealed with heavy fabric-backed tape. I picked at the tape and it nearly fell off into my hand, the adhesive long dried to a crumbling powder. Unwrapping the oilcloth, I found four small black ledgers of American origin. They were about five by eight inches, and excellently preserved. I opened the top ledger and found that the first 16 pages had the top 20 lines filled in. On the 17th page, only the top seven lines were used. The filled in lines contained only an American (or English) name, the first three lines on page one reading "Young, James Thomas", "Wood, Robert Winston", and "Burton, Charles Gordon".

I picked up another ledger, and opened it to find that, like the previous book, the top 20 lines on the first 16 pages were used and the 17th page had only the top seven lines filled in. The difference was in the notations themselves, which consisted only of numbers. The numbers seemed entirely random, running from three to five digits.

The third book had precisely the same pages and lines used, but listed only the names of cities or communities. The leading three lines read, "Norfolk, Virginia", "Denver, Colorado", and "Groton, Connecticut". I was becoming puzzled at how the sparse notations in these ledgers could have been of such importance as to warrant an armed courier carrying them to Russia.

The last ledger furnished the only connection with Russia so far. Its lines were filled in with Russian names, the first three of which were, "Barkov, Fyodor Lukich", "Glushkov, Nikolay Kirillovich", and "Shcurov, Aleksey Ivanovich".

'Well,' I thought to myself, 'Jim McGann's gotta know more than I do about this spy stuff. If he thinks these books are important enough to risk my ass for, I'll treat 'em like they're gold. But if they're not, I'm gonna kick his butt.'

I rewrapped the books, replacing the useless tape with a spare bootlace I always carried in my hunting pack, and spent the next 20 minutes concealing the package.

CHAPTER 20

The Satisfaction of Finding Her

When I got back to the plane, Neeta was perched on the trailing edge of the wing, a safety rope looped around her waist, reading through a stack of 30-year-old magazines. I could hear Mike rummaging around inside the cargo bay. I climbed aboard and joined him.
"Anything of interest?"
He stood up from the wood crate he had been prying at with the crash axe.
"No surprises," he said. "About what you'd expect. Crates of military barbed wire, rolls of commo wire, cases of spark plugs, tactical radios, machine tools, hand tools, cases of 50 cal machine gun ammo and half-dozen guns to fire it, lotsa' bolts of wool cloth and rolls of canvas—looks like the contents of a quartermaster warehouse."
"No boxes of gold, diamonds, rubies, or pirate treasure, huh? Looks like we wasted our time."
"One thing of interest," he grinned, "I found three cases of condoms. Looks like the Russkies had big plans for the occupation of Germany after they took it."
"That or they had a shortage of weather balloons. Anything else that might interest us, or the intelligence people?"
"Spam." he said. "Case after case of Spam. They must really love that stuff."
"I've heard that it's real popular in a lot of foreign countries," I said, "but I'm not sure I'd try the 30-year-old stuff. You didn't

find any 30-year-old booze, did you?"

"Now that you mention it, there's a case of bourbon with several bottles unbroken in case you want to celebrate tonight."

"Hell, yes! Bring 'em along. We can sample one to make sure it's still good—then give a bottle each to Red Buckner and Jim McGann as souvenirs of our trip. But for now, it's getting toward chow time. Let's leave everything we found back where we found it—except the bottles, of course. I don't want anything in our camp that might tip people off that we're on the wreck."

"Expecting visitors?"

"Maybe. The way McGann acted, he thinks the Russians might find out about it and try to make a claim. Might use force, even. He thinks the briefcase is really important to them, even after 30 years."

After another hour of poking around in the cargo bay, we shut down for the day. We were getting less light from the sky, and I didn't want to use up all our flashlight batteries our first day on the job. We returned to camp with only our rifles, packs, the three surviving bourbon bottles, and a few old magazines that Neeta wanted to look through. I buried two of the bottles in some loose sand near the lake shore and put the third with Mike's scotch bottle for future attention.

We took our time cleaning ourselves up and rearranging camp to suit our current whims. With the evening meal selected ('dinner' to my non-southern comrades, 'supper' to me), we leaned back against the sitting log and cracked Mike's scotch bottle. Conversation was quiet, mostly speculation concerning World War Two, the men and women who fought it, and the tools they used.

"I wonder how many more wrecks like this one are scattered around Alaska, just waiting to be found?" asked Neeta. "A lot must have been lost with the kinda' weather we have. Even now, we lose a bunch every year."

"Jim McGann told me a lot about what went on," I replied, "and I did some reading on the subject. Over 8,000 airplanes of various types were flown from Grand Forks to Alaska and on to Russia from '42 to '45. About 700 were C-47s, like our Red Starred Lady.

"According to official figures," I said, "we lost 133 over Alaska and Canada. Not C-47's necessarily, but all types combined. And I'm sure the Russians lost a bunch over Siberia that we'll never know about."

"What do you think is in that briefcase that our intelligence people are so anxious to get?" asked Neeta. "After all these years, there's not much relating to War Two that hasn't come to light. And all that old technology is obsolete."

"I doubt that it's related to technology," I responded. "It has to be something that, if revealed, would embarrass some government, or would mess up somebody's long-range political plans. The Russkies tend to plan a few wars ahead, you know. They were thinking about stirring up North Korea long before 1950 when the war started."

"How would we know that?" asked Mike.

"Well, for one thing, North Korea was fully equipped for war using Russian arms, Russian tanks, Russian communications gear, and the latest Russian MiG jet fighters. That's not a logistical feat than you can get done in a year, or even two, considering you have to train the locals on how to use, maintain, and repair all that new stuff.

"Hell, when World War Two ended, Korea had been taken and occupied by Japan for over a generation; it was a subservient nation with no real military establishment to build on. But they were damn professional when I was fighting 'em. I expect Russia had been working 'em up since '45, when Japan surrendered." I hoisted my rear up onto the log and extended my cup toward Mike, who had current custody of the bottle.

"Another two fingers, if you please, then I'd better start my C-rats a'heating." He emptied the bottle into my cup—not quite two fingers worth—and put the bottle in the carry-out trash bag.

The "C"s tasted good after a long day of climbing in and around the C-47. Long-unused muscles were complaining, both to Mike and to me, judging by a certain stiffness of movement around the camp. Neeta, on the other hand, seemed as spritely as ever. Youth and clean living, I supposed. Wasted on those who appreciate it least.

"I can see why you like those C-rations and In-Flights." she commented. "No work involved, and no dishes to clean up. I think we ought to try 'em next time, Mike."

I smiled with the smug satisfaction of one-upsmanship. I had long ago settled on "C"s where weight was not an issue. I carried a small aluminum pan which I filled with water and set over the fire. I dropped the can or cans into the water until hot, fished them out, opened them, and ate. The hot water in the pan was used for the instant coffee or cocoa provided with the ration. Clean-up consisted of burning out the used cans in the fire, then burying or packing them out, and pouring the left-over pan water on the fire when done.

After supper, we lazed around, pulling on jackets against the evening chill but still comfortable around the small fire.

"What's left to do?" asked Mike. "We have the briefcase. I don't think there's anything in the cargo bay that we can haul away in Red's Cessna that's worth the trouble. In fact the whole cargo, while interesting, isn't worth hauling out piecemeal. Maybe, if a heavy-lift helicopter could jerk the whole plane free and drop it in Anchorage intact, it would be of interest to some war museum somewhere. Otherwise, all we have is the satisfaction of finding her."

CHAPTER 21

Bottled in Bond

We slept longer than usual, having no major challenges weighing on our minds, so it was late Tuesday morning when we climbed up onto the wing of the Red Starred Lady. We devoted the morning to a rough inventory of her contents, although some of the crates held hundreds of mechanical or electronic items which, not being labelled, defied identification. If the equipment or machinery for which they were intended was now obsolete, their purpose would probably never be known.

There were some electronic components which were obviously parts of early avionic radar equipment, and which were just as obviously hastily ripped out of their normal mountings. I suspected that Russian procurement specialists were not above stealing classified equipment from American planes if it could not be gotten any other way.

We avoided the forward section of the plane where the bodies of the crewmen moldered away, entombed for a generation. I was unsure what to do about them—my experience with human bodies had always been with fresh ones, and with the carrying or burying of same. I didn't think there was any way to remove these from the flight cabin with decorum or dignity. Ripping them from their present location, more-or-less glued to the structure of the aircraft, and tossing them out of the cabin windows, would probably result in a pile of fragments and scraps on the ground below. The stream bed was near bedrock—there would be no grave digging there, and carrying arms full of body parts out to more welcoming ground was not in my plan for the day.

I asked Mike and Neeta about their thoughts on the matter, but they seemed to prefer not to deal with the subject. I decided to go along with them and to defer the decision for another day.

Having started our chore late in the morning, we put off lunch and worked until mid-afternoon, then quit for the day. As we were packing our gear to return to camp, an odd feeling struck me. I turned to my partners.

"Just on a weird hunch—let's take down our ropes and ladder, and any other signs of our work here. If we do have visitors, it might be good if they had no hint that we could have already found the briefcase."

First, we bent the flap of aluminum back up and into place, covering the hole Mike had cut. It wanted to spring back out, of course, but a thin tube of aluminum broken from the interior wall and slipped between the flap and the frame served to retain it in place.

I unfastened the ladder from around the aileron and flipped its top loop over one of the propeller blades that jutted out at a slightly higher than horizontal angle. Moving very carefully, I untied both ends of the safety line from their anchor points and passed an end around the aileron. Pulling it through, I used the doubled line as a safety rope until I had worked my way down to the top rungs of the ladder. When in a reasonably secure position on the ladder, I took one end of the safety line and pulled the other up and through the aileron, coiled it in my hand, and dropped to the ground below.

I descended via the ladder with relative ease and joined the pair below. It was an easy matter to walk toward the tip of the propeller blade while flipping the ladder until it worked its way out over the tip and dropped to the ground.

We walked back and forth, peering up at the wreck from all angles, but could see nothing which betrayed our presence. Neeta pointed to the two rocks which had anchored the ladder. I nodded, and Mike and I returned them to their previous beds near the stream.

Satisfied with a job well done, we walked back to camp carrying the climbing gear with us. As the other two began retrieving the food sack for the evening meal, I went out from camp a hundred yards or so and hid the ropes, ladder, and crash axe in the brush. Now, if we did get unwelcome visitors there should be nothing to suggest that we had breached the wreck and carried off any sensitive matter. That might stave off trouble for a while, anyhow.

When I returned to camp, I asked Neeta if she thought a bottle of bourbon would get better or go bad after sitting for 30 years.

"Why Ben," she answered, "that's the kind of question that could try the patience of philosophers for half a century, wreck friendships, confuse scientists, and possibly start wars."

"Well, then," I replied, "the only way to find out would be to test it. Mike, are you brave enough to give it a try?"

"Hell, it couldn't hurt much more than falling off a wing that's 30 feet in the air. I've risked that in the name of science, so why not risk being poisoned by antique bourbon?"

He pulled the old bourbon bottle from his stuff bag and held it up to the light.

"Nothing's moving around in there, and if it was, I could probably choke it down if the booze was good. Let's give her a try."

I took it and examined the label. It was a plain label reading "Old Ren", with no fancy gold embossing or flamboyant seals, and it displayed a picture of a magician pulling a rabbit from a hat. A hundred proof, according to the label, and bottled in bond by Squibb in 1944. A cheap-appearing label in my opinion, and nothing to get excited about, but what the heck? The price was right.

I handed it back to Mike who opened it and doled out three fingers for each of us. My first sip made me out a liar. Although I was not a bourbon drinker, I knew this was special stuff. Too sweet by some standards, it had grainy nuances and a vanilla background which stayed with me long after the first swallow was long gone.

I waited for the others to sip, watched the smiles appearing on their faces, and asked, "Whatcha think?"

"Ben," said Mike, "to hell with Red and Jim. This stuff is going home with us!"

Neeta nodded vigorously in agreement.

"OK," I said, "but let's try to make this bottle last us a while—at least until we're picked up. That'll leave a full one each for celebrations later."

CHAPTER 22

Vertical Butt Stroke

Between us, we evidently didn't have all that much will power. We buried the empty bottle in the gravel the next morning with military honors. Then Neeta and I each took a remaining bottle and stashed it in our stuff bags, wrapped in laundry against accidental breakage.

There was nothing much to do on the wreck, and we weren't ready or willing to tackle the disposition of the crewmen, so we took our time with breakfast and camp cleanup. It was nearly 10 o'clock when Neeta first heard the sound of a helicopter making its way down the valley. Mike's hearing and my own had long ago become dulled due to constant noise exposure, but we picked up on it soon after.

The noise faded, then returned, louder, and we were able to see the chopper heading southward toward the head waters of the Gerstle. A few minutes later, it returned, much nearer to us and flying northward. It was obvious now that the bird was flying a search pattern, and I was afraid I knew the object of its search.

The machine suddenly took an abrupt turn and headed straight for us, descending as it did so, and levelled out near enough that its rotor wash began wreaking havoc with our once-orderly camp. I stepped out into plain view and waved it off, rifle in hand. The sight of the rifle seemed to get their attention—the pilot sliding his machine north about a hundred yards and setting it down at the edge of the lake, pointing toward us, the right skid in the water and the left high and dry on the gravel. I could see by the commercial logo on its side that the chopper belonged to a flight service at Merrill Field that specialized in renting and leasing light aircraft.

The air blast from the rotor had carried away everything loose that had been in our camp. Mike's tent, securely pegged down, had withstood the man-made gale, but my new outside-framed tent had popped loose and cartwheeled merrily up the beach, coming to rest in a scrub willow thicket.

Neeta began angrily chasing down the camp gear that had been blown away while Mike and I walked toward the helicopter, whose rotors were winding slowly down to a stop. We both carried our rifles under our arms, pointing generally forward but not directly at the chopper.

"Don't threaten," I told Mike, "but let them see that we're ready. I'll do the talking, but butt in if you think it's important."

A door opened on the shore-side. Two men got out, attached a small set of steps, and stepped respectfully aside at the emergence of an older man in a smartly tailored civilian suit. His dress was in contrast to the first men, who were in identical, and apparently new, camouflage-patterned hunting garb. He strode forward, a smile on his face, and met us 20 or so yards from the chopper.

I saw a tall dignified man in his 50's, well dressed, wearing a butch haircut and a small version of a Joe Stalin moustache. He put out his hand more-or-less between Mike and me, a subtle way of finding out who was in charge. When I took it, he swung his attention to me.

"Good morning, gentlemen. I am Dmitri Shelikov, Second Secretary to the Assistant Soviet Ambassador to your United States."

"My name is Hunnicutt; this is my partner, Michael Gearhart. What can we do for you, now that you've destroyed our camp and interrupted a peaceful morning?"

My tone was deliberately severe—I didn't want him to think we were impressed, either by his elaborate title, or by the sudden emergence of four other men from the door of the helicopter. The six men, now walking up behind their leader, were similarly dressed, the original two wearing sidearms, the last four cradling AK-47 Kalashnikovs.

The four new men didn't look right to me. Their urban appearance and grooming, the unsteady way they picked their way across the rocky beach, and the awkward way they handled their weapons, reminded me of fresh-from-the-city recruits at boot camp. The first two, however, could have been their drill sergeants. One bearded, the other clean-shaven, they exuded arrogance and barely hidden hostility.

"I apologize," smiled Shelikov, "and my pilot will answer to me for his carelessness. Shall I have my men assist in putting your camp in order?"

"No thanks," I said, "and again, what can we do for you?"

"It has come to the attention of the Ambassador that a Russian aircraft has been discovered in this area. I have been ordered to come here and take possession of it for my government."

"Well, Sir, according to the International Laws of Salvage, it no longer belongs to your government. We'd be pleased if you'd take your people and move along so we can go about our business."

Shelikov visibly stiffened, his polite smile instantly vanishing.

"Mister... Hunnicutt, was it? In 1944, that aircraft was officially turned over to the Soviet Union at your base at Great Falls, in Montana. It became our property at that time, and it was on its way to Russia, flown by a Russian crew, when it disappeared. It is irrefutably our property."

Shelikov spoke nearly perfect English, a mere trace of accent to be heard. I noted that as he became angry or frustrated, the accent became thicker and more easily identified as Russian. That would be an interesting tell in a poker game, and I tucked the thought away against future need.

"Mister... Shelikov, was it? There were hundreds of C-47 airplanes, American, Russian, and Canadian, flying these skies. Dozens were lost, both during and after the war. How can you be so sure this one was Russian?"

"The tail number," he replied, "The original transfer paperwork noted the tail number, which corresponds to the number on the wreck."

"And how could you know that? Have you seen the wreck? Have you read the tail number? Do you know its location? And, if so, why aren't you on it instead of harassing us?"

He grew red in the face, started to speak, then stuttered into silence, not wanting to admit that there were Russian agents in the FAA or our military.

It was at that moment that Neeta joined us, standing quietly by Mike's side. The bearded Russian took immediate notice, whispered to his partner who whispered back, making a sign with his hands that obviously referred to Neeta's tiny size. The bearded one laughed, made a comment out loud, and clapping his left hand to his right bicep, shoved his right forearm upward behind his clenched fist, an unmistakable phallic gesture.

Neeta, rifle in hand with its butt trailing in the dirt, moved to face him at arm's length. He laughed again, and made a short suggestive remark in Russian.

It was hard to follow her movement, so quick and unexpected was it, but the rifle butt left the ground and slashed upward. The sound was like an axe thudding into a chopping block, the momentum seeming to lift the Russian inches into the air, as the rifle butt buried itself in his crotch.

Without doubt, it was the most beautiful example of a "vertical butt stroke" I had seen since Infantry Basic Training.

CHAPTER 23

International Diplomacy

Concurrently with the bearded one's high-pitched squall, his partner started toward Neeta. He was instantly stopped by two rifle muzzles jabbed into his chest, and a sharp "Nyet!" from Shelikov. I was not sure which was more effective, but his sudden freeze undoubtedly saved his life. Mike and I had loaded our rifle chambers when the helicopter landed.

The four unseasoned Russians had not moved during the episode, and were obviously unsure as to the proper response. Shelikov motioned to the nearest pair, pointed to the moaning victim, and waved toward the helicopter. The designated pair rushed forward and dragged the casualty toward the aircraft, their weapons dragging and bumping along the ground. Definitely rookies.

"I must apologize again, it seems. As you see, I did not have a wide selection of helpers from which to choose. Although your reaction was rather extreme," he nodded toward Neeta, "I suspect he will learn from it. If nothing else, he will know that explosives can come in small packages." He added a smile at his little joke.

He turned back to me but I interrupted before he could open his mouth.

"Your people are unusually well armed to be on a diplomatic mission?"

He searched his mind for an answer.

"We were told there were many bears in these mountains."

"Oh, yes," I replied. "There have been several near camp, both black bear and mountain grizzly. As you can see," I hefted my rifle, "we always go armed and ready for instant defense." I sincerely hoped he would get my point.

"Let us drop the question of how I know the tail number of the C-47."

His voice was nearly without accent now; I assumed he had control of his emotions and was thinking clearly.

"Let us assume I am correct concerning the number—and you know that I am. I can produce credentials showing that I represent the government of the United Soviet Socialist Union. I can also produce official papers proving the delivery of this airplane to our government in 1944. I can even show you a copy of the cargo manifest. Legally, then, you must convey custody of the plane to me."

"Sir," I said, "with all due respect, you've ignored my mention of the international laws concerning the rights of salvors. When a ship or other craft becomes an abandoned derelict, and its owner or insurer makes no attempt to recover it, salvage rights may accrue to an outside party who does so. My party, whose work you interrupted, is conducting a salvage operation."

"But we did not abandon the aircraft, Mister Hunnicutt; we searched but could not locate it. We have now located it through your efforts, and we will establish ownership and possession."

"Well," I replied, "there is a saying in the legal community that possession is nine points of the law. I must point out that we have possession and you don't."

"There is another saying," he answered heatedly, his accent thickening, "that might makes right. I must point out to you that my might exceeds yours by almost three to one—and one of yours a woman."

His accent was very pronounced now, and his face growing red. I just might have goaded him a step too far. I had no wish to push him into a fire-fight under these exposed conditions, so I took a step back.

"Sir, I think it best we call a timeout for lunch and further thought. Why don't you come into our camp in an hour for a diplomatic discussion of our mutual problem?"

He stood for a few moments digesting my suggestion.

"And", I added, "I am a former officer of the Army and I

understand the conditions of a truce. You will be safe and free to leave our camp—and this valley—at will."

His face relaxed, twitching a bit at the phrase, "and this valley". He smiled and put out his hand.

"In an hour." He did a sharp about face and motioned his men back to his helicopter, joining them at its door.

My crew returned to our camp.

Mike, Neeta and I sat around the cold fire pit and munched on our preferred noonday snacks—mine still consisting of Baby Ruth bars, while Neeta enjoyed a healthier nut bar and Mike stole from her at every opportunity.

"Neeta, were you really trying to start World War Three by decking that poor bastard?" She threw me a pitying look.

"Ben, if you knew what he said, you'd have done the same; not as well as me, of course, and that probably would have started a war."

"You knew what he said?"

She sighed, moved to where she was facing both of us.

"You both might as well know. My full name is Renata Durova. My parents were of the Russian aristocracy, and had to flee Russia after the 1917 revolution. The Bolsheviks were slaughtering everyone connected to the ruling class—even their servants. My parents fled separately, but met in California in the 1930's and married—I was born in 1940. Although they had both learned English when young, they spoke Russian around our home. I don't speak it as well as I should, but I understand it. That bearded bastard should have had his tools amputated instead of compacted!

"Anyhow, I took the single name 'Neeta' because a budding artist has to have a distinctive and memorable name to get ahead, especially in San Francisco where there are a million budding artists."

"Have you heard anything from our Russians that we need to know?" I asked.

"No, your boy Dmitri has done most of the talking, and in English."

"Well, keep your ears open, and don't let on that you understand 'em. That should give us a leg up if they get to yakking among themselves."

"What are we gonna do, Ben?" asked Mike. "If they get rough, we could only get about half of 'em, what with the AK's. Maybe we ought to give 'em the Lady since we already have what they're looking for."

"That's about what I had in mind. But we can't give in too easily—we can't let 'em suspect that we've already been aboard and gotten the briefcase, and if they search the wreck, they'll find that out."

Our conversation was interrupted by the sight of Dmitri Shelikov striding across the gravel toward us, a forced smile on his face.

CHAPTER 24

A Visit to the Lady

"Come sit." I invited, making room on our sitting log. Shelikov joined us, keeping a respectful distance from Neeta.

"Mister Hunnicutt, we seem to be at cross purposes in this matter. I would ask you to consider it from my point of view. We know exactly what is, or was, in the cargo bay of the aircraft. I would be happy to show you a copy of the manifest so you can judge its value for yourself. Believe me, it is not of such value that you would profit by salvaging it. In fact, it is very unlikely that my government would decide to salvage it."

"Then, why are you so anxious to take it from us?" I asked.

"You were a soldier," he replied, "so you may understand. There were four of my countrymen aboard. We wish to either repatriate their remains or, if that is not practical, to give them a fitting burial here."

"I understand," I said, "but we have a considerable investment in this project. It would be hard for us to just write it off and leave the wreck to you."

"Have you been aboard the wreck?" he asked, with a touch of strain in his voice. I laughed.

"Sir, if you had seen the wreck, you wouldn't ask. It seems inaccessible, although we've developed some ideas of how to get into it. Expensive ideas."

Shelikov sat silently, his face contorted in deep thought. Finally, he raised his head and reluctantly looked us in the eye, one at a time.

"Would you show me the airplane? If it is situated in as difficult a spot as you say, I may be able to offer a solution that will satisfy both of us."

I gave Mike and Neeta a questioning look, accompanied by a slight nod of my head. They nodded in return.

"We will show you the plane, but we don't want your comrades along. Another incident like this morning's could cause serious problems."

"Agreed. I will go and give them instructions before we leave. How far is the wreck from here?"

"That depends on how fast you walk, naturally, and if you are in condition for a steep climb. It could take two hours. We'll walk over to your helicopter with you; we can start from there."

Shelikov was visibly unhappy with this provision, but gave a small smile of understanding as he stood and waited for us to get our gear and follow him.

He called his people to the door of the chopper and informed them in Russian as to our plans. The bearded one, standing with his thighs unnaturally far apart, glowered at us all, fixing his gaze primarily on Neeta. His partner appeared unconcerned, and the four rookies wore their usual air of confusion. I glanced at Neeta and she gave a slight nod which I took to mean there was no trickery afoot.

We struck out for the Lady, Shelikov appearing to brace himself for an extensive hike. After 15 minutes of walking, I stopped the group. Shelikov looked at me questioningly; I grinned and pointed straight up. When his gaze followed my finger and he saw the Lady looming above, his sharp intake of breath was audible.

"Not very accessible," I commented.

"No," he agreed, "and I can see why you have not yet boarded her. There appears no feasible way without flying in some specialized equipment and cutting a road into the forest."

He examined the Lady from several angles, my party holding its collective breath lest he spot some sign that we had been aboard. He abruptly turned to me.

"From the lack of extensive damage to the fuselage, the cargo would be mostly intact, and the remains of the crewmen still in the flight cabin."

I nodded in agreement.

"What is your estimate of the value of the ship and its cargo should you succeed in salvaging it?"

"Frankly, Mister Shelikov, we have no real idea. The cargo might just barely pay for the salvage operation, but the overall value would depend upon just who might want to buy it. There are rich collectors who spend hundreds of thousands restoring World War Two airplanes which would actually be worth much less except for their historic value.

"For instance, a millionaire who flew the Lend-Lease route during the war might spend half a million due to his personnel connection with that project. And even pay the cost of a heavy-lift helicopter to haul it out to Anchorage or Fairbanks. A large museum might be willing to pay $50,000 for the plane and cargo to display in its present condition as a tribute to Russian-American cooperation and sacrifice during the war. Some government agency would probably foot the bill for that.

"We're gambling—we really don't know what the payoff might be."

Shelikov walked down to the stream and took a seat on one of the rocks which had anchored our ladder during our climbing exercises. After five minutes of deep thought, he stood and approached.

"Gentlemen, Lady, consider this. After seeing its location, I will recommend that my government make no attempt to physically move the airplane. Our entire concern now relates to the honorable disposal of the remains of the crewmen. Since it is impractical to remove those remains, I intend to dispose of them by burning, in the manner attributed to the early Vikings. My men will assemble here for a proper ceremony, to which you are invited if you wish to attend."

That suited me right down to the ground—if it burned in place, the Russians would never know that we had taken the briefcase from the flight deck. It wouldn't do, however, to agree too easily; we had to take the role of greedy Americans.

"I object! Our time and money are deeply involved in this project. We sympathize with your desire to honor your countrymen, but we can't stand aside and watch you burn our plane." I emphasized the "our".

"We should return to your camp to discuss the matter," said

the Russian, still in his calm no-accent voice. "After all, it is only two hours of hard climbing." He gave a wry smile.

"It was clever of you to exaggerate the distance in order to discourage my men from following us and exerting undue influence."

"I did say that it would depend on how fast one walks; you, Sir, are a fast walker."

CHAPTER 25

The Last of the Lady

Our arrival at camp interrupted what appeared to be an illicit gambling game, judging by the haste with which the men disbursed from a small huddle near their helicopter. The bearded one, however, casually came to his feet stuffing money into his pockets. His challenging expression defied his boss, or anyone else, to criticize his behavior. His partner watched, as usual, seemingly unconcerned with what was happening. I was becoming interested in the partner, obviously a veteran, and with an air of leadership about him. He was tall, dark, and good-looking in a Gregory Peck sort of way. His voice, though seldom heard, was deep; his words slow and decisive.

Shelikov ignored them and led us to our own camp and to the sitting log.

"I agree that you should be compensated for your discovery of our aircraft—he emphasized the word "our"— and for any possible profits you may lose. My superiors anticipated the possibility of such a situation, and provided me with certain funds for that purpose.

"Would you consider a one-time payment, for which you would sign—I think you call it a 'quit-claim'—and concede all rights regarding the wreck to my government? This would remove all complications and prevent possible future problems with your own government."

I sat silent, appearing to consider the proposition, although in my mind it was a done-deal at any price. Neeta spoke up.

"What figure did you have in mind, Dmitri?" Her injecting herself into men's business seemed to shock Shelikov, as well as her casual use of his first name. He quickly recovered and glanced at Mike and me. While we sat silent, awaiting his reply, he recovered and responded.

"Somewhere between the value suggested by your imaginary millionaire and its actual value, as is, and where is. How about $50,000?"

"A generous offer," I said. "That takes care of me. Now how about my two partners?"

"You value your find highly, Mister Hunnicutt. You must think there are many millionaires who are searching for a wrecked, inaccessible Russian cargo plane."

"I know of only one plane that's on the market, Sir, so it might be considered a seller's market. And I must ask, how did you plan to pay for this exchange?"

"I brought cash, Mister Hunnicutt, against just such a situation as this. You can all fly back to civilization much wealthier than when you came here; was not that the intent of your mission?"

"If we can each fly out $50,000 wealthier than when we came, Mister Shelikov, I think we may have a deal." I glanced around at my partners, each of whom nodded. We all turned our attention to the Russian.

He appeared reluctant, but I could see he was relieved to have finally struck a deal which removed all obstacles to the completion of his mission. He put out his hand to each of us.

"I would like to organize a ceremony to honor the crew of the aircraft, and to burn the wreck. You are welcome to attend. Then we can consummate our deal back here at your camp and we will leave you." He saw doubt in some of our eyes.

"You may trust me. And if you have doubts, you have your rifles—I am sure I would be the first target."

"How do you plan to burn it?" I asked. "There will be little or no fuel in the wreck; the wing tanks went with the wings, and anything left would have long since evaporated."

"We knew that there was a possibility that, for any number of reasons, we might need to destroy the plane. I obtained a compact version of a military flame thrower which should serve to ignite the magnesium and aluminum components. The plane will burn.

"I will detail two men to stay with our camp when we go to the wreck for the ceremony. Protocol, you understand. We have a certain amount of sensitive material in the helicopter." He turned and began giving orders to his men.

I moved to one side near Mike and Neeta.

"He's telling the two vets to search our camp to insure we don't have the case," she whispered.

"That's great," I answered. "I want them to be damn sure we don't."

She looked at me questioningly.

"Don't worry," I said. "They won't find it."

An hour later, the Russian group was gathered 50 feet in front of the nose of the Red Starred Lady. Shelikov called them to attention and delivered a short talk in Russian. My crew stood respectfully behind the Russians and patiently listened, although Neeta was the only one who understood. When he had finished, the Russian summoned a man carrying a large pack containing several cylinders joined by complicated plumbing.

He fiddled with the various valves and hoses and warned everyone back. Shelikov moved his group another 50 yards back from the plane, faced them about, and called for a salute. The Russians executed a snappy salute, holding it while he snapped an order to the flame operator. My group saluted also.

A fountain of orange flame erupted from the nozzle of the flame thrower and rose like the water from a fireman's hose, enveloping the aircraft in a sheet of flame. After five or ten seconds the fire began to subside, its initial fuel having burned off. The operator loosed another fire stream, holding it longer and concentrating on the main hull and cabin. As the second dose of flame began to die, the kindling point of the structure was reached and it began to flare. The flare was encouraged by another stream of fire, and soon the entire plane was an inferno.

Above the roar of the flames, we heard a sharp command from Shelikov and his men dropped their salute; we followed their example. I looked up at the Lady, her red stars now swallowed by fire, and saw a slight movement.

I cupped my hands and shouted to Shelikov.

"Move your people back! She's coming down!"

I turned and hustled my crew back another 30 yards. As the

heat of the fire cooked the wings and the main wing spars, they softened and began to give, to bend upward, releasing the plane from the grip of the canyon walls. With a loud groan and a crunching sound, the entire aircraft crashed to earth, sending out bits of glowing metal and fiery sparks. A cloud of steam burst forth where the white-hot metal was quenched in the cold running stream below.

About that time, the heat worked its way through the wood crates and inner steel containers of 50 caliber machine gun ammunition which made up part of the cargo. The cartridges began cooking off, causing some consternation until we realized that they had little more effect than firecrackers when not confined in a weapon's chamber.

The movement to the rear had come just in time; even so, several men cursed and danced when struck by hot sparks and flying metal. Shelikov ordered one more stream of fire into the flight cabin, insurance, I thought, against any fragment of the briefcase or its contents ever coming to light.

Within half an hour, the C-47 was a blackened mass no more than five feet high, its surviving structural members standing out like the ribs of a decayed whale carcass. The charred starboard engine lay to one side, a tombstone for the grave of the Lady. A few last cartridges cooked off, and the wreck made small ticking sounds as it began to cool.

CHAPTER 26

A New Russian Revolution

We returned to camp a little saddened by having to watch the death of the ship we had gotten to know so well. It felt good to have confidence, however, that now the Russians could never know that we had their secret cache, whatever it might turn out to be.

That smug feeling abruptly left me when we broke out into the camp area. I saw the two camp guards standing, each with one of our bourbon bottles in hand, grinning at us, the bearded one leering at Neeta.

Shelikov saw them also and broke into a torrent of Russian that would have done credit to a drill sergeant of any nation. The bottles were both two-thirds empty, but the two miscreants adamantly refused to surrender them to their boss.

"I am very sorry," he said to us. "I would offer to replace your whisky, but I allowed none on this mission for the very reason you see. Did you have the bottles in view?"

"They were well hidden," I replied, "so your men must have searched our camp in detail. On your instructions, I assume?"

Shelikov didn't answer, but turned away and walked back to the Russian camp. He noticed that the flame thrower operator had dumped his unit near the fire before searching through the supply cache for a bite to eat. A sharp reprimand followed, and the fire unit was placed under a tarp well away from the campfire.

We retired to our camp and set about readying our evening

meal. We had been active enough, and were hungry enough, that C-Rations and MRE's were starting to taste reasonably good. In fact, at this stage, I considered anything in a can—anything that wasn't concentrated or freeze-dried—to be pretty damn good. I got my water boiling in the pan, dropped in an olive drab painted can stenciled "Pork & Beans", then added another for good measure. I ripped open the packet of "Coffee, Soluble" and emptied it into my cup, ready for the hot water when the cans were done.

Mike and Neeta were preparing their MRE's for heating when Dmitri Shelikov appeared, slogging toward our fire, his face downcast.

"I don't know how to apologize enough to you. My men acted badly today, not that those two have ever been angels. I will replace the whisky with some choice vodka when we return to civilization. Where shall I send it?"

"Mister Shelikov," I replied, "considering your line of work, I'm sure you can find out exactly where I live. I'll be looking forward to sampling some really good vodka.

"Just don't have it delivered by your bearded friend," I added. "I'd hate to have to hurt him."

"Never underestimate him," Shelikov said, "One does not become a senior sergeant in the Russian army by being kindhearted. Nikolay Gushkov was recently broken to private for the near-murder of a Polish police officer who interfered with his dalliance with that policeman's daughter. His continued existence is due only to influential friends in political circles."

"Thanks for the heads-up on that issue," I said. "What about our compensation for the C-47 that you destroyed this afternoon?"

"In the morning, if you please. Gushkov is still drunk and obstreperous; I suspect waving around a large sum of money might trigger another incident. I hope you understand my problem. Most of the other men with me are clerks and helpers around the embassy—I cannot depend upon them to stand up to him if he rebels against my authority."

"Then I hope to see you in the morning. I'd invite you to share our supper but, as you can see, it's only military field rations. You won't be leaving before settling up with us?"

He chuckled and waved at our rifles, all propped within easy reach.

"If you hear our helicopter start up in the morning before I pay you, you have my permission to open fire. I would prefer you hit the engine rather than my people, but do what you think best. I plan to visit you after breakfast."

With that, he turned back toward the cook fires of his own camp.

We turned in early that evening, Mike, and I sitting guard and relieving each other at four-hour intervals. We didn't much worry about being attacked, but were concerned about having thieves about camp during the dark hours. We were awakened around seven in the morning by the chatter of voices in the Russian camp, so roused out and started our Spartan breakfasts. About the time we finished cleaning up, we saw Shelikov approaching with a large satchel, not unlike the briefcase we had just high-jacked. We waved him over to the sitting log and took our places beside him.

The Russian produced a clipboard from the satchel with an official appearing paper in several copies attached. He handed a copy to each of us to read. It was indeed a form of quit-claim, and clearly stated that all rights to C-47, tail number 92943 were waived and it was acknowledged that the aircraft and its entire content were property of the government of the U.S.S.R. to do with as they desired.

"I have directed that two of my men, embassy clerks, not the two soldiers, witness your and my signatures and the transfer of the compensation." He gave a small smile. "If there is any suspicion whatsoever that I might have profited from our arrangement, I might disappear."

He waved two of his rookies over to our fire. As they stood to comply, Gushkov and his partner also stood, brushed the rookies back to their seats, and took their AK's from their hands. Thus armed, they strode across the opening between the two fires and approached us.

I saw Mike change the position of his Weatherby for more ready access, Neeta doing the same for her Winchester. I stood, hands in pockets, facing the intruders, and rearranged the little Smith & Wesson 38 so that its grip was cozy in my right hand.

Shelikov, anticipating trouble, waited until the menacing pair was close before voicing an order. He snapped out a volume of Russian which could probably be translated to, "Stop and get your asses back to camp!" He signaled the remaining four to converge on our camp, and on the double.

Gushkov turned about, casually chambered a round in the AK he was carrying, and just as casually fired a long burst from the hip in the general direction of the advancing Russians. I was sure he meant it only to halt their advance and send them scurrying back to their fire.

Unfortunately for all concerned, at least two of the blindly fired bullets took effect elsewhere. One found its home in the right leg of an oncoming crewmen, who staggered and fell. The other emitted a solid ringing sound as it punctured the pressurized cylinder mounted on the frame of the flame thrower. Mike started to reach for his rifle, but Gushkov's partner threw a round in the chamber of his own AK and held us in place.

Shelikov roared a command in Russian, but was ignored. Two of the rookies grasped their downed comrade under the arms and dragged him toward the helicopter. And the damaged flame thrower began a firework display that put the cremation of the Red Starred Lady to shame.

CHAPTER 27

Rebels on the Run

Liquid under pressure spewed from the punctured cylinder like water from a fireman's hose. As the spray contacted the campfire, it ignited with a dull 'whoomp', turning the vicinity into a fountain of fire which enveloped everything in its range. At first, the helicopter was outside this range, but as the flames heated the cylinders on the flame thrower, pressure built up and the fire fountain blossomed.

A crewman, the pilot, I assumed, dove through the door, and ran forward in an attempt to start the aircraft and move it clear. I thought I heard the engine cough once or twice, but then liquid fire completely enveloped the machine and it burned at an unstoppable rate. I didn't see the pilot again.

The two unwounded rookies hastily moved their tents and equipment out of the danger area. One then tended the wounded man while the other stared despondently at the remains of the helicopter, now cooking in the fire of its own ruptured fuel tanks.

With both the ex-soldiers standing by with automatic weapons, there was little we could do but watch the helicopter burn. I guessed that many of their supplies and food stores were still aboard and being consumed by the hungry flames. That should lead to interesting confrontations when we all got hungry again—we had brought a few days' extra chow in case our pick-up plane was weathered out, but certainly not enough for us and a squad of hungry Russians.

Shelikov was white-faced and silent, staring at the two rebels with the gaze of an executioner. The silent one stepped over, collected our rifles, and emptied them, dumping our cartridges on the ground. Gushkov picked up the money satchel and they both moved a safe distance from us. Gushkov opened the money satchel and I could hear the sharp intake of breath from both as they saw the amount within.

While they were entranced at the sight of the cash, I could possibly have drawn the 38 from my pocket and shot them both. I considered trying it, but the 38 Special is not really an instant knock-down cartridge, and one surviving pissed-off opponent with an assault rifle can kill a lot of people before he discovers that he has been fatally shot. I chose to wait until the chances of carrying it off were more in my favor.

Besides, there was something disturbing about the thought of cold bloodily shooting down a pair of men who were not an immediate threat. I had nearly done so in the past, and was not proud of the fact.

After searching through the satchel, Gushkov and his friend returned to where we had all resumed our seats on the log. Gushkov had a triumphant look on his face while his companion seemed to be in deep thought.

"You have more drink?" Gushkov asked me in a hoarse voice.

"You know we don't," I responded. "You searched our camp."

He looked sorrowfully at the now empty bottles which he and his friend had carelessly tossed on the ground.

"Not matter. We rich—buy all we need later."

When his friend spoke, I was surprised to hear an English which was as good or better than that of Shelikov.

"Comrade Shelikov, Nikolay Gushkov and I have decided to enter upon early retirement. The funds," he indicated the now-closed satchel, "which you were about to give these profit-seeking Americans should allow us to live quite well in whatever location we might choose."

"Alexei Shilov, you are a traitor and a thief. You will be hunted, captured, and probably executed. Do you really want to end an honorable career in such a way?"

"Dmitri, be careful. I can easily give Nikki and myself an additional advantage by killing all here. By the time our authorities and the Americans have determined what happened, if they ever do, we will be in another country."

"Would you do this?"

"I would prefer not to. If we leave with government money, we will be pursued, assuming our government does not decide to just bury the matter. If we leave with the money, and with seven dead bodies behind us, the pursuit will be vigorous and never-ending. Please do not force us to take the latter choice."

I spoke up. "How do you intend to leave? If you wait for our chartered plane, you'll have immediate questions to answer, and you'll be put down in the middle of Anchorage."

He mulled the question over in his mind for half a minute. I noticed that he made no attempt to consult with his partner—it was likely that he had the same regard for Nikki Gushkov's wisdom and intelligence that I did.

"The map that our pilot used to navigate—it showed this place as being on the Gerstle River. The river flows north, does it not?"

I nodded an affirmative.

"How far north, if we followed the river, until we encounter a major road?"

"My charter pilot told me that, in an emergency, I should walk north to the Alaska Highway. He said it was about 20 miles."

Alexei smiled, motioned Gushkov to one side for a private conversation.

Dmitri Shelikov turned to me with a puzzled look on his face. "You are helping them escape? You could have lied and sent them in the wrong direction."

"Yes," I said, "but if they died lost somewhere in these mountains, it's possible that nobody would ever find them—or our money; I want to know where to find both.

"By the way, how much more cash was in that bag than the $150,000 that was due us?"

"There was a total of $200,000." he said, "If we had to buy your rights to the wreck, we wanted to be sure to offer enough. You Americans have a reputation for being greedy." He said this last with a small smile which somewhat softened the insult.

The two vets joined us. Alexei laid out their plan.

"We will walk north. It will take a day and a half. We will take food for three days. This will leave you short, but today is Thursday, your pilot comes Sunday. A little hunger will do you good. By the time you return to Anchorage, we will be beyond reach of the authorities."

The two rebels wasted no time. Alexei left Nikolay Gushkov to guard us while he scrounged through both camps to accumulate the rations he needed. When he returned with two well-filled packs of rations and gear, he looked over our rifles with interest. My 338 was a bit battered from my fall on the rock slide. Neeta's was serviceable but well used. Mike's 300 Weatherby was near new, with a glossy stock, several fancy inlays, and a large deluxe Weatherby scope sight.

"I will take your fancy rifle," he told Mike. He faced the rest of us.

"We will leave the remainder of the rifles with you," he said, "but we will remove the bolts from your rifles, and from the crewmen's AK's. We will leave the bolts in some prominent place a kilometer or two on our trail—I wouldn't want you eaten by bear after we go."

I reached into my jacket pocket and produced a full box of 338 Winchester ammunition.

"Here," I said, handing it to him. "You may meet a bear also."

He tucked it into his own coat pocket with a smile; then sent his partner out to collect rifle bolts.

"I hope I shall only need it for bear," he said. "But you should know that I will shoot anyone who follows us."

He waved Gushkov over and they went out of our hearing. As they checked their gear and supplies, Gushkov appeared to be arguing about something, Alexei adamantly shaking his head, no. Gushkov pressed the matter, motioning toward Neeta. My hand went back to the little 38 in my pocket, this time no doubts in my mind about shooting, if it came to that. Neeta wasn't blind to the developing situation—I saw her move a little closer to the small camp axe we used for gathering firewood.

Luckily (probably luckily for Nikolay Gushkov), Alexei prevailed and the pair left camp, walking north along the east side of the Gerstle flood plain.

CHAPTER 28

Huey

Alexei was true to his word. A pile of rifle bolts was arranged on a large log about a mile north of the camp. I brought them back to camp, retaining the ones for the AK-47's and putting mine and Neeta's back in our respective Winchesters.

"Ben," said Mike, "what the hell? You gave that guy the wrong ammunition!"

"Really?" I asked. "Damn, I musta' been nervous as hell, pulling a dumb trick like that. What do you think might happen if he tries to shoot it?"

"Well, it'll go into the magazine OK, and it'll probably go into the chamber if he really pushes on the bolt. But when you try to fire a 33-caliber bullet in a 30 caliber bore, it'll probably…"

"Yep," I said, "it probably will."

"You sonuvabitch! That oversized bullet'll build so much pressure trying to squeeze through the bore that it'll rupture the cartridge case and maybe blow up the gun."

"Yeah, and it would be a shame, blowing up that pretty Weatherby of yours. But he'd only get one shot, and I doubt that the deformed bullet will hit where he's looking. I'm not too worried about Gushkov's AK—we've seen how well he can shoot. But Alexei taking one of our scoped rifles did worry me. He could pick me off at a quarter-mile with any of them. I was sorta glad he picked the fanciest one; hoped he wouldn't check the ammo too close when I handed it to him."

"OK," he said. "I guess I can sacrifice the Weatherby for a good cause. Does that mean we're going after them?"

"You heard their plans. Do you think they can make 20 miles in a day and a half?"

"More like three days—if they're lucky," he answered. "They'll have to cross a dozen side creeks that feed the river, and maybe pick their way through or around log jams, beaver ponds or mud slides. Plus, if they're fresh off the streets of Washington DC, they won't be in the shape they think they're in."

"My thoughts exactly. But I wouldn't try to chase 'em. If they started a day ahead of me, they'd likely get to the highway a day ahead of me and be out of reach by the time I catch up.

"If our pick-up comes in early enough Sunday, Red'll be able to fly me up to some lake near the Gerstle River Bridge where I can either intercept them or notify the Alaska Troopers. They could check-point the Canadian border and the Fairbanks airport—the most likely escape routes. Then he could come back here and fly this crew back to Anchorage."

"You're gonna go after them alone?"

"Well, do you wanna leave Neeta here alone to handle this crew?"

"I see your point," he said. "But if I stay, there'll be four Russians and Neeta and I. Can Red's plane carry six?"

"I think so if all the gear is left behind. Nearly half his fuel will be gone—that'll shave a lot of weight. If he can't, leave a couple of the Russian crew behind and send back for 'em later. They'll survive."

Shelikov had been a silent bystander during our conversation. I could see that he realized he was no longer running things, but he seemed to bow to those with knowledge of the land and the resources available. He stepped forward.

"Please send my wounded man out first, if you must divide our group. The two remaining will be alright for a day or two, though probably frightened half to death." He gave one of his characteristic half-smiles. "Being alone in this country is like being alone on another planet if one is not accustomed to it, and my men are creatures of the city.

"And I should go out first to alert my ambassador of the events of this mission, and to receive any further instructions he may have for me."

I searched his words for trickery of some sort, but had to

agree with his reasoning. I nodded.

"Sounds logical to me." I handed him an AK-47 bolt. "They'll feel better with a weapon, and there are full magazines in all the AK's. Just caution 'em not to shoot a bear unless it actually threatens 'em. An angry bear can do a lot of damage before it decides to die.

"And," I continued, "tell me more about Alexei. He's no ordinary embassy gofer—in fact, I'd bet he was sent to look over your shoulder."

Shelikov hesitated a moment, then opened up.

"You are correct. I would not say this were he still loyal, but Alexei Shilov is probably a KBG agent assigned to assure my proper conduct, and to collect intelligence wherever he can. I would have considered him an outstanding example of patriotic loyalty to Mother Russia. But it seems that wealth and a life of ease in a less oppressive locale have overcome his love of country."

"Do you think that both he and Gushkov will survive their journey?" I asked.

"I believe only one will complete the trip, and with all the money." He hesitated for a few seconds. "Mr. Hunnicutt, you should reconsider your plan to follow them and retrieve the money. Gushkov is an animal; his own wants and pleasures rule him, and he will kill on a whim. Shilov is quiet, intelligent, and as deadly as an asp when he must be. You may find that the money in that bag is not worth risking your life for."

"Thank you for your advice, Sir—I'll keep it in mind." I wondered at the strained voice in which Shelikov delivered his advice, but assumed that the stress of command was beginning to have its effect.

I walked over to the sitting log and sat, mulling over our plans, and trying to foresee any serious surprises that might pop up. Shelikov joined his remaining troops and gathered them by their ever-present fire to explain their future.

As it turned out, all our planning for the exodus was unnecessary. Late the next morning our routine camp chores were interrupted by the distinctive heavy "thump, thump, thump" familiar to most US soldiers as the sound of an approaching UH-1 "Huey" helicopter. The Huey, painted the typical US Army olive drab, was flying a search pattern along our side of the river plain. It suddenly veered off its course and beelined toward our camp, settling down on the opposite side from the burnt-out shell of the Russian-chartered machine. I noticed that it was a gun ship with a cluster of motor-driven Gatling-styled barrels protruding from a housing near the nose, and that it had been landed with the barrels aligned on the Russian camp.

When the waist gunner's door opened, a familiar gangly frame emerged and trudged across the gravel toward me.

"Damn!" said Jim McGann, waving toward the burned-out chopper. "You didn't start a war with 'em, did you?"

CHAPTER 29

The Hunt

"Jim, we gotta' talk." I led him to a private space away from both camps and sat him down on a handy boulder.

"First," I said, "we got your briefcase. Second, the other side doesn't know. Third, the C-47 has burned, so they'll never know from us."

I then brought him up to date in detail, finally asking him what the heck he was doing here.

"My outfit got word that a Russian official with diplomatic papers had leased a chopper out of Merrill Field," he explained. "I didn't know their intentions, so as soon as I could get the Army off its ass, I arranged to get a Huey and come out here to see if you were in trouble. Sounds as though you and your friend are OK except for losing the ransom you pried out of Shelikov. That's what you get for being greedy."

"Greedy?" I said, "Hell, we have to supplement our income somehow, what with that measly pay you're giving us. There's nothing of the plane to salvage and sell and we didn't find any gold in the creek; we had to extract our pay from the Russkies."

"Well, that's gone now. You might as well get used to being poor again."

"You think so? Buddy, before you ferry these folks back to Anchorage, you're going to Huey me to the Gerstle River Bridge on the Alaska Highway. I'm gonna collect what's due us, then turn any survivors over to you."

"Ben! Damn your stubbornness, I can't just use a government

aircraft to set a vigilante down in the bush to whack a couple of foreigners."

"No, but you can make points by placing a contract agent in position to capture a pair of foreign agents who are armed and loose on American soil."

I led Jim over to the Russian camp and introduced him to Dmitri Shelikov, identifying him only as a representative of the US government. Shelikov informed Jim of the official reason for the Russian expedition and Jim pretended to believe him.

"Unfortunately, one of my men, in a drunken rage, wounded another and destroyed our sole means of transportation. I would be greatly obliged, Sir, if you would arrange a rescue for us. My government will gladly reimburse yours for any expenses incurred."

"I am glad you were able to provide an honorable disposal of the remains of your World War Two air crewmen. And my helicopter is empty, except for me, my pilot, and my gunner." He emphasized the word "gunner" slightly as a reminder of who was now the dominant party.

"We will be able to transport your people and my own back to Anchorage as soon as I have delivered Mister Hunnicutt on an errand of his own. Is there someone in Anchorage who can take care of your needs and see to the care of your wounded man?" I admired the dexterity with which McGann traded his conversational slang for the precise official English of a bureaucrat.

Shelikov assured Jim that there was such a person; I had no doubt that person would soon be on the list of possible foreign agents under surveillance by Jim's CIC cohorts.

While all concerned parties were reorganizing and collecting their gear for travel, I led Jim back to the screened latrine trench we had dug when we had first arrived. I pointed to the stake I had punched into the ground to prop up the shovel.

"The briefcase, mostly intact but rotted, is about a foot down under that stake. There is a Russian service automatic in the case also. It is fully loaded and may be shootable— be careful how you handle it. The case will be hard to smuggle onto the Huey unnoticed, but the four small ledgers inside would fit under a coat. You could take them now, or later."

I walked away leaving him to make his decision—and, more important to me, shedding all responsibility for the case and its contents.

In less than an hour, I had accumulated the gear I would need for my hunting expedition. Since I planned a waiting game, I didn't worry about packing light. I took the best of the available rations, my warm leather flying jacket, a sleeping bag, and a small foldable camp stove and fuel bottle that I found in the Russian camp. No need to signal my presence to Alexei with an open fire and wood smoke. I actually figured Alexei to hit the highway late tomorrow, but not knowing his rate of travel, or how much of his time might be lost in a disagreement with Gushkov, I prepared to stay in the field three more days if necessary.

Once buckled into the rear compartment of the Huey, gear checked and rechecked, I asked Jim to tell the pilot to fly over the opposite side of the range from the river. No use giving Alexei any clue that he might be greeted at the highway. The Huey, making all the usual Huey-type noises, lifted, spun around 180 degrees, and surged forward and upward, away from our multi-national camp site.

We reached the Alaska Highway in 15 minutes or so and turned westward toward the bridge. The pilot settled the chopper near a wooded knoll about a mile short of the bridge. He was as quiet about it as he could manage, but there is no such thing as a quiet Huey. I bailed out, waved at Jim McGann and the pilot, and slipped away into a little plot of scruffy black spruce.

When the racket of the helicopter had faded to a distant heartbeat, I took stock of the terrain. I saw clumps of spruce, soggy moose meadows, and a homesteader's shack on the opposite side of the road. No traffic was visible at the moment. I shouldered my pack, now too damn heavy to carry very far, and struck out for the bridge.

CHAPTER 30

Wait and Watch

The Alaska Highway is the only road into or out of Alaska. One would think that it would be heavily travelled, but on this particular Friday, traffic was light. During the 15 minutes it took me to reach the bridge only two vehicles passed, neither stopped. Tourists, I assumed, as Alaskans nearly always stopped to ask a traveler if he needed a ride or help of any sort. Today, that suited me—I wasn't interested in drawing attention of any kind.

When I was a hundred yards from the east end of the low bridge, I left the road and moved down into cover beneath the abutment at the end of the bridge. Dragging out my old Zeiss 10X40 binoculars, I spent a solid 20 minutes minutely examining the flood plain and the wooded area on the east side of the river. Nothing moved, or drew my attention.

The river, at this point, was made up of many smaller braided streams intertwining through the sand and gravel of the flood plain. Scrub brush was growing in many places where small islands had formed, and old logs and root wads dotted the plain. The bridge system was about a third of a mile long where it crossed the gravelly river bed; the bridge itself was a low-lying truss structure made up of steel girders and beams.

At first, my scrutiny detected nothing, the broad valley floor desolate and lifeless. Then a flicker of movement—a coyote stalking unseen prey, one hesitant step at a time. A thicket stirred and gave forth a moose cow leading a calf toward a low spot containing pooled water. A fat bear waddled out from behind a hummock a quarter-mile away—no, not a bear, but a fat yellowish porcupine, similar in silhouette but much nearer than I had guessed.

Continued watching revealed other life—the coyote's target, a family of ptarmigan scratching in the river gravel; a few parka squirrels scurrying about on a low mound well above the high water mark on the river's bank; a single wolf on the top of a rise on the far side of the Gerstle, who seemed to evaporate into nothing as I watched.

I could be sure man hadn't disturbed the river bed lately or the various inhabitants wouldn't still be going about their daily business. But I knew my guestimate of the Russians' progress could be way off for a dozen reasons, and I preferred to be over-cautious in dealing with them. I arranged a minimal camp using the walls of the abutment as shelter and the road above as a roof. To screen my lair from view by an observer from the south, I cut away some scrub brush and tried to place it as a natural-appearing copse facing south.

It was late afternoon by the time I had prepared my little fort to my liking. I had stopped and scoured the area every half-hour since I started, so it was unlikely that the two Russians could take me by surprise. Nevertheless, a feeling of being watched haunted me throughout the remainder of the day.

I had had such feelings before when hunting dangerous game, whether two or four legged, and I knew it was mostly fueled by my imagination. I thrust the feeling aside and prepared to get comfortable for the night. Night travel in this country was dangerous, mostly because the various unseen hazards. Slippery logs, unseen potholes, sinkholes in the beaver ponds, or undercut stream banks could cripple a man as effectively as an encounter with a grizzly. Most cross-country trekkers were happy to establish camp while it was light enough to do so.

By full dark, which came late at this latitude, I had finished the meal that I had heated on the Russian camp stove. The stove turned out to be of Swedish manufacture, probably purchased in Anchorage when Shelikov outfitted his crew. It was remarkably light and efficient, and the Swedes being neutral, I figured it was as much mine as anyone's—I doubted it would ever find its way back into communist hands. Such was my greedy logic, anyway.

I also gathered grapefruit-sized rocks from the river bed

below and placed them on both sides of the abutment so an intruder couldn't climb up to my nest without kicking some loose and causing a warning clatter. The essentials taken care of, I wrapped my tired body in my bag and immediately fell asleep.

I was wakened early by a noisy magpie croaking and chuckling around my little fort. I tried to be annoyed, but it was full daylight and past time for me to start checking the river plain. I thanked him, or her, and had a fried Spam breakfast. The Spam had come from the Russian camp, and I recalled the many cases of it that we had found on the Red Starred Lady. The Russians must really like that particular Capitalist contribution to the world's hungry. I did, myself.

My morning view to the south revealed nothing significant, just the same wildlife drifted to new areas for their foraging, and apparently undisturbed by humans. The air was cool in the mornings, so I found sunny spots to sit and scan, slowly moving every few minutes to follow the sun. These less-than-extreme bursts of activity were occasionally interrupted by an involuntary nap, which was itself interrupted by the movement of a restless sun, leaving me again in the chilly shade.

The afternoon eventually turned warm, whereupon I varied my routine (and avoided naps) to a schedule of scanning the plain for ten minutes of every hour, and walking back and forth on the hidden north side of the road bed for exercise. Except for movements of the wildlife out on the river bed, the only events breaking the monotony were rumblings overhead as the occasional car or truck crossed the bridge.

It was mid-afternoon when one of my strolls was rudely interrupted by the clatter of automatic weapons fire to the south.

CHAPTER 31

A Blind Hog

I shamefacedly picked myself up out of the dirt. Old reflexes had kicked in and I'd plowed face-first into the ditch on the north shoulder of the highway. Even before my belly hit the gravel, I knew the shooting was far enough upstream that it couldn't have been intended for me. I scuttled back to my hidey hole and brought the binoculars into play.

There was no repetition of the shooting—the only difference in my view of the river plain was the sudden absence of wildlife. Man had come, and wild things fled or hid. I stayed still, binocs at ready, waiting for the next development. The adrenalin which had fueled my reaction to the gunfire slowly dwindled away, leaving me trembling a bit but with slightly sharpened vision and an intense desire to end this game quickly while I was sure I could win it. Such overconfidence often came with an adrenalin rush, at least in my case, and I knew I had to guard against its leading me into trouble.

I watched over the area for a good 20 minutes before detecting any sign of motion. Just as I was about to lower the binoculars and give my eyes a rest, a tiny movement behind a screen of scrub willow caught my attention.

I concentrated on the willow clump and waited a further five minutes. The movement occurred again—an arm reaching ahead and clawing backward, pulling a human torso behind it. The torso raised itself until the head could view the ground ahead, lowered, and an entire body was revealed crawling slowly toward the bridge but taking advantage of the cover of every bush and rock.

All the Russians were garbed alike, so I couldn't tell if it was Nikki Gushkov or Alexei Shilov I was seeing. I silently watched as the man crawled from bush to depression to rock to log, always in the direction of the bridge. It soon became obvious that he was primarily concealing himself from anyone behind, rather than anyone viewing from the bridge.

As he neared my position under the bridge, I was able to catch his face in full light of the sun—no beard; it had to be Alexei. Spots of blood became visible on his clothing as he neared; I couldn't tell where he was hit, but all four limbs seemed to be in use. If this meant he was body-shot, he was in trouble. My doctoring skills were pretty well confined to patching arms and legs.

I suddenly wondered why I was concerned about treating his wounds. After all, I had made this journey for the express purpose of shooting him if necessary.

As I followed his progress, I had also been watching his 6-oclock, concerned that Gushkov might be trailing him for a finishing shot. I found it interesting that I had picked the wrong Russian for the role of the victim. I had assumed that Alexei's intelligence and his planning skills would make him the sure winner in a contest of treachery. It would seem that Nikki Gushkov had somehow caught his partner off guard and sprayed him down with a typically unaimed burst from his AK-47, grabbed the money satchel, and headed toward the bridge or highway on his own.

Which made my situation tenuous, to say the least. If Nikki wasn't behind Alexei, he must have struck straight for the highway through the brush cover on my left. If I went out to help Alexei, I was a sitting target for any shooter up on the road bed. If I didn't, Alexei was the sitting target whenever Nikki broke out of the wood and spotted him—or us.

Alexei appeared unarmed, although he might still have the Russian service pistol he had worn earlier in the week. This meant that Nikki might have an AK, the scoped Weatherby, his own service pistol, or all three. My own armament consisted only of my scoped Winchester rifle and the little 38 revolver in my pocket. If I went out to Alexei, I would probably be beyond the range of Nikki's pitiful marksmanship, barring a lucky shot. Thinking back to the Russian rookie and the punctured flamethrower, I had to admit that Nikki was good at lucky shots. Of course, he might use the scoped rifle, which I hoped was still booby-trapped with oversized bullets.

'No use overthinking the matter,' I decided, snatched up my Winchester and left my little fort. I dog-trotted the hundred yards to where Alexei lay in a depression behind a half-buried log and plopped down beside him. Alexei had been scrutinizing the plain behind him and my arrival was completely unexpected. He reached toward the pistol at his belt, but I clamped down on his arm with one hand and removed it from his holster with the other. Then I twisted around and checked the bush and roadbed where I guessed that Nikki might be. Nothing.

"How bad?" I asked in his ear, still watching for Nikki.

"A graze on left hip," he replied, "and a bullet in left shoulder. A ricochet, I think. I can feel the bullet under the flesh."

"Can you walk or run?"

"I can walk, I think. Was just crawling to stay out of sight—I think Nikki's behind me somewhere."

"Not to second guess you, but if he shot you down, grabbed the money, and disappeared, I'd figure he'd just head for the highway looking for a ride, and leave you here to bleed."

He looked at me, puzzled to himself for a few moments, and slapped himself sharply in the head.

"Certainly! My mind must be muddled. In fact, it has to be or I would not have given Nikki the opportunity to surprise me."

"We can talk about that later. I need to get you up under the bridge so I can plug your leaks, and we have to do it before Nikki spots us and pins us down here in the open."

The immediate response to that logic was a burst of AK fire which kicked up dust and dirt over a half-acre of flood plain, but short of us by 40 yards at its closest. I rolled over and spotted the shooter up on the shoulder of the road, probably 200 yards up the road from the bridge. Another burst of fire achieved the same results, the closest bullets being random ricochets over our heads. Our boy evidently didn't believe in using the range scale on his AK sight.

They say that even a blind hog finds an acorn once in a while. I had no intention of being that acorn. I unslung my Winchester and snapped off the piece of tire inner tube I used as a lens cover. I took a rest on the log we lay against, caught Nikki in the field of the scope, and centered the crosshairs high on his chest. By rough artilleryman's calculations, the hypotenuse of the 100-yard, 200-yard right triangle we formed, which would be my shooting line, was around 220 yards. I was zeroed for 200 yards. Just as I slid a round into the chamber, my target dipped nearly out of sight. I steadied my rifle as he stood again; this time he was holding Mike's Weatherby. I could see his hold was wobbly and he held the rifle awkwardly, so stayed off my trigger for a time.

I knew my delay was stupid, that I was just curious to see if the booby trap worked, and was willing to risk another lucky shot to find out.

CHAPTER 32

Murder

As I watched through my own scope, Nikki Gushkov touched off the Weatherby. There was a spasm of smoke, small parts flying through the air, and Nikki jumping and gesturing as though someone had thrown boiling water in his face. The shrill keening of the mutilated bullet splitting the air above us told me that that particular rifle was unlikely to threaten us again.

Nikki picked up the AK, fumbled a fresh magazine into the receiver, and wildly unleashed its entire contents in our direction. We kept low, neither wanting to be the blind hog's acorn. I hugged the earth as tightly as I could, and would have gotten lower yet if my buttons hadn't gotten in the way.

When the sound of battle had died away, I put my safety on and tried to decide what to do next.

"Does he have any more weapons?" I asked Shilov.

"A pistol, I think. You can easily kill him before we get into pistol range." He nodded toward my Winchester.

"But what happened to his rifle?" he asked. "It seemed to blow up in his hands."

"I think he used the wrong ammunition," I said, not wishing to explain that Shilov himself was the one for whom I had intended the booby trap. He would figure it out in good time.

I turned my attention back to Nikki. His attention seemed to be focused on something in the distance; I began to hear a sound, a vehicle approaching from the east.

"Oh, damn!" I stood and began running toward the bridge.

"He'll highjack that car; maybe kill someone."

As I ran, Shilov shuffling along behind in obvious pain, I could hear the vehicle begin to slow. Gushkov was probably waving it down, his face and arms bloodied by fragments of the blown-up rifle, and the driver— in the Alaskan tradition— would surely stop to help. I cursed myself for not killing him in cold blood when I had the chance.

He was on the far side of the highway now, awaiting the vehicle and out of my view. If he hurt or killed someone, there would be another link in the chain of guilt that I somehow seemed to accrue over the years.

The vehicle slid to a stop, a blue pickup truck judging from the top of the cab—all I could see of it from my position down on the river bed. We could hear the murmur of voices which rose in volume to a shout, then the "pop, pop" of a pair of pistol shots.

By now, I was within 50 yards of the scene, mostly still invisible from below the road grade. Gushkov suddenly appeared, dashing across the road, and bending out of sight to retrieve his pack and the money satchel. I took quick aim at the place I thought he would reappear and touched the trigger at the first flash of movement.

I had misjudged—the bullet missed his head by a matter of inches, and by the time I had cranked in another cartridge I heard the truck door slam. Gushkov slammed the truck into reverse and floored the accelerator, the truck careening down the highway backward and fishtailing as he sought to maintain control.

By the time I had scrambled up the bank onto the road, the truck had stopped, turned about in the road, and was accelerating eastward. I saw a figure sprawled in the roadway near us, a red stain spreading from it. I wanted to fire on the truck cab, now barely within range, but held back for fear that there might be another innocent aboard.

Alexei and I examined the figure in the road, an elderly woman in farm clothing, quite dead. She had been shot in the chest and the throat and dragged out of the cab onto the shoulder of the road. There was nothing to indicate whether or not she might have had a companion.

I knelt beside her, rigid with fury at Gushkov, at myself for not having stopped him when I could, and at the state of mankind that allowed and encouraged such outrages to take place.

I looked over at Shilov to see his reaction, wanting to tar him with the same evil brush that painted Gushkov. To my surprise, his face was a picture of pain and anger, not unlike my own. Alexei muttered a few words in Russian, delicately closed the woman's staring eyes, and stood up, looking eastward.

"We must kill that bastard," he said. "He will do this again, and worse." He looked over at me with sympathy in his eyes. "Yes," he said, "you should have killed him earlier, but you were not to know this would happen. I would have done so, because I know him well."

We moved the body well off the road and arranged her in a position of dignity. There was no identification of any sort on her—we assumed that Nikki Gushkov had taken any purse or wallet she possessed before leaving her in the dirt beside the road.

I looked at Shilov's wounds; he had cut a sleeve loose and used it to bind the leg wound before beginning his crawl north. It seemed to serve, and there wasn't much bleeding, so I adjusted it a little looser to allow circulation. The shoulder wound was, as Alexei had guessed, caused by a misshapen bullet which looked to have ricocheted off a rock and buried itself an inch deep just in front of his left armpit. I could feel it under the flesh, much to Alexei's discomfort.

"I could probably get this out," I said, "but I'd need something like a sterile set of needle-nosed pliers. Otherwise, I'd just get the bullet out and let infection in."

"We will wait," he said through clenched teeth as I probed the skin around the wound. Which suited me fine—I hated doctoring people.

Gushkov had left an empty AK-47, the blown Weatherby rifle, and several empty AK magazines. I examined the Weatherby; its bolt was half open and bits of melted and blackened brass were plastered inside the receiver. The barrel had a swollen lump just forward of the chamber where the tight 338 bullet had built up far more pressure than the action could handle The brass cartridge case which normally provided a seal against hot powder gasses had melted and flowed, allowing the gases to enter the action and vent through every opening. The stock encasing the magazine had splintered, probably sending slivers of walnut and hot brass into Gushkov's arms and face. If the bullet had not swaged down enough to exit the bore, it was likely that the entire breech section would have exploded like a hand grenade—and solved our current problem.

CHAPTER 33

Hard-Hearted Angel

"Alexei, where would he run to? What were your plans when you grabbed the money and walked north? You must have had some plan for hiding or getting out of the country?"

"Nikki had vague ideas about working our way to an airport where we could fly south across the border to Mexico. His idea of heaven was lying under a warm sun, drunk, with a woman waiting on him."

"And your little heaven?" I asked.

"Your own Alaska is very like a part of Russia where I grew up. I had thoughts of fading into the population here, living quietly, possibly raising a family. I love my country, but not what she has become."

"Well, we'll have to talk about that later—right now, I have to catch or kill your buddy Nikki. Do you think he'll try for Canada, or for an airport and a plane south?"

"Nikki Gushkov is a creature of whim. He will drop a good plan in an instant if another seems better for any reason. He also believes that enough money can buy anything. I think he will head for Anchorage and a flight to wherever seems most inviting at the time."

"Would he take a hostage?"

"Any hostage Gushkov might take should be presumed lost. He would use a woman until she made him angry, then kill her just to keep others from enjoying her. He would hold a man just to dominate or humiliate him, or to use him as a shield. He might then kill him if it were not too inconvenient, or just throw him out of a moving car—or airplane.

"You must understand that Nikki is a very strong, very aggressive child with no moral concepts that do not include his own pleasures and comfort. I have had access to his personal file and—if I did not need him—I would kill him like a snake."

"A high recommendation," I commented dryly. "He must have been a nice guy to travel with."

Shilov started to reply, but I shushed him. A new sound filtered into our ears, a vehicle, this time coming from the west.

I moved far enough onto the bridge to halt the oncoming vehicle well before the driver could see the murdered woman lying on the shoulder of the road.

"Alexei, you keep quiet until we find out what we have to deal with here. I won't mention your place in all this yet, but we have some talking to do later."

He nodded soberly and took his place near the body.

The vehicle was an aged but well-cared for GMC pickup with a striking non-factory yellow paint job. It ground to a halt far enough away from me that the driver would have several options if he didn't like what he saw. One, of course, would be to back quickly away, retreating westward across the bridge. The more likely was to floor the pedal and run me down before I could use my rifle.

My rifle! Dammit! I had intended to lean it against the rail out of easy reach, so as not to alarm the driver, but it was still cradled under my right arm. I hastily cached it and walked around to the driver's window.

The driver was revealed to be a large, very healthy blue-eyed blonde woman who eyed me suspiciously as I approached.

"Pardon me, Ma'am, do you live around here?"

"Depends on your definition of 'around here'. I live about 40 miles that way," she hitched a shrug behind her, "and I'm headed about 50 miles that way." She pointed east.

"We've had a carjacking and a murder here," I explained. "We have no transport and need to catch a ride to report it to the Troopers at Tok."

She quickly opened the door and slid to the bridge surface.

"Who was killed?" she asked, moving toward the body that

she could now see by the roadside.

I gulped loudly before coming up with a "We don't know." The gulp was nearly a gasp. Before us stood a fair imitation of the kind of blonde Nordic goddess who would have occupied all of Adolph Hitler's erotic dreams. Over six feet tall, she was bigger than life in all respects, but was well enough proportioned that everything fell together quite nicely. Her face was handsome, not beautiful, and with far too much character in it to be termed 'pretty'. Most men would have to stand on tip-toe to look into her eyes, and I thought the view would be worth it.

She was wearing bib-overalls, a faded grey flannel shirt, and lace-up work boots. As she moved toward the body, I could see the outline of a small automatic pistol tucked into her right hip pocket. There was barely enough room.

"Oh, Lord! It's Sherry Jensen. What the hell happened?"

"A long story, ma'am. We were pursuing a thief. He ambushed us, shot my partner here." I motioned toward Alexei's bloody wounds. "While we closed in, this lady came along in a blue pickup, so he shot her and took the truck toward Tok. This is what we found."

"You can't just leave her here for the birds," she flared. "We'll put her in the back of my truck and take her to Tok."

I expected the Troopers to have something to say about screwing up a crime scene, but we could always blame it on her insistence. While Alexei helped arrange poor Ms. Jensen in the truck bed, I hastily rolled up my camp and its gear and loaded it also. We collected the left-over guns, making sure that the Amazon was a witness to what we picked up, and to the scattered AK brass strewn around.

The blonde made a cursory examination of Alexei's wounds and decided nothing more could be done on the scene.

"Ride in the bed and look after Sherry," she ordered. "No need of bloodying up my cab."

Having firmly established that she was no Florence Nightingale, she motioned me into the right seat, climbed behind the wheel, and peeled out toward Tok.

CHAPTER 34

Tok

The driver's features were quite tense for a while, but she eventually relaxed, reached across the bench seat, and shook my hand.

"I'm Margaret Gibson. I work a small farm just out of Delta. You are..."

"Ben Hunnicutt, retired Army. I'm doing some contract work for the government right now. Sorry we got you mixed up in this, Miss Gibson."

I had immediately noted the lack of any rings, but thought it discreet to confirm her status. I was fated to be disappointed.

"Mrs. Gibson," she corrected. Then atoned somewhat by adding, "My husband died in a bush plane accident almost eight years ago."

"You farm by yourself? You must keep busy—any farming is hard work, and you're a slave to the land, the livestock, and the weather."

"You've been there?" she asked, glancing at my relatively uncallused hands.

"Long ago and far away," I replied, "as a boy in Virginia. Tell me about Sherry Jensen."

"Lived in a used-up homestead near me. Raised enough in her truck garden to feed herself—I took care of a couple of pigs for her winter meat. She was probably on her way back from shopping at Tok when that bastard shot her." She turned and stared at me, the truck roaring unguided down the highway.

"You'll get that killer." It was an order, not a question.

I tried to keep the conversation going but, after glancing once through the rear window at the body, she withdrew into herself. I couldn't much blame her, so I used the silent time to muse about my relationship with Alexei, and how far I could trust him.

We had no real interaction with him until he and Nikki had openly mutinied against Dmitri Shelikov. I suspected that Alexei had planned for a while to part company with the Soviet Union, and the availability of the money triggered his decision. Nikki Gushkov, on the other hand, was probably motivated exclusively by the money—and possibly by veiled suggestions from Alexei.

Alexei had not evidenced any brutality, had left the weapons bolts so we would not be helpless, and seemed to have convinced Nikki to leave Neeta behind.

For a villain, he was too good to be true. Even now, he was riding into the arms of the law, evidently trusting me to protect—or denounce—him, as I saw fit. And I had to admit, there was probably nothing he could be arrested for. A Russian national with diplomatic ID, his only crime was getting shot by another Russian national with diplomatic ID. The money was Russian owned—we had never signed the quit-claims—so what was his crime against the United States?

His status in regard to his own nation was considerably different. He had announced to his countrymen that he was defecting and that he was taking their money with him. In my mind, a self-imposed death sentence. We badly needed to talk at the next opportunity.

I awoke from a doze as Margaret steered the truck off the road and into the parking lot of the Alaska State Trooper Detachment headquarters in Tok. She and I left Alexei with the body and entered the headquarters building. I was uncertain where to go, but the lady seemed to know her way around. She waved me to wait at the desk and headed down a hall to the offices. In less than a minute, she was back with a Trooper Sergeant in tow. I followed them outside and we showed the Sergeant the body and provided a brief explanation of the circumstances.

The expected flurry of excitement died down after the Sergeant gave the necessary orders for temporary disposal of the body, and made sure that Margaret Gibson, Alexei, and I were available for detailed questioning and statements. A Trooper was dispatched to the Gerstle River Bridge with a camera and evidence gathering equipment, and a call made for a medic to come and look after Alexei. I button-holed the Sergeant, showed him the special blue-tinted Federal ID that Jim McGann had issued me, and asked if I could brief him in private. Evidently the ID carried some weight, as the Sergeant took me into a room with only two chairs and a small table, sat us down, and ordered that we not be disturbed.

The Sergeant's name was Jordan according to his nameplate; I introduced myself and slowly gave him a sanitized version of the events surrounding the Red Starred Lady. He seemed a bit put-out that all this, including automatic weapons fire and the burning of two aircraft, could take place on his watch without his knowledge. In order to better establish my bonafides, I referred him to a Trooper John Smith with whom I had worked on several occasions, mentioning the fact that two years ago, he was working out of the Glennallen Detachment. I also gave him Jim McGann's contact information.

Sergeant Jordan excused himself, ostensibly to fetch us some coffee, but I was sure he was going to contact Trooper Smith to verify my sanity. He returned eventually with two cups of nearly cold coffee, confirming my suspicions.

"Mr. Shilov believes that Gushkov's present goal is Anchorage," I said," and that he's looking for a flight or boat in the direction of Mexico. But Gushkov is somewhat stupid, is unpredictable, and makes decisions on the spur of the moment. We can both attest to the fact that human life means less than nothing to him."

"I have an all-points out for him and the truck," said Jordan, "and designated him as armed and dangerous. I think we can stop his leaving Alaska, but if he holes up in some homestead or cabin, we might never locate him until someone is reported missing or dead."

"Well, about all I can tell you at this point is that he's not bright, speaks poor English, is easily distracted, loves booze but can't handle it, and he's a piss-poor shot with an AK-47. I think he's only carrying a Russian service pistol right now. And neither Gushkov, Alexei, nor I have eaten in a good while. Is there a place nearby where we could chow down? And I'd like to buy the lady dinner for helping us out."

"Sure," he said. "The Tok Roadhouse is close. Don't count on buying Peggy dinner or a drink, though. She's been fending off the local men for years, and makes sure she never gives 'em an excuse to stake a claim." From the rueful smile on his face, I guessed that he may have been one of the prospectors.

"One other thing," I said. "I think Nikki Gushkov will try to stock up on booze sooner rather than later. I'd start checking out any place he could buy or steal it. Might get an early lead on where he's heading. And," I reluctantly continued, "when his gas gets low, he'll hijack or steal another vehicle. Let's hope he can steal one—if he hijacks one, he'll probably kill the driver on general principles."

CHAPTER 35

Love and Barley

The Tok Roadhouse served roadhouse food as good as any I had sampled in the state. Not fancy, but well-prepared and piled high. Margaret, or Peggy as she was called locally, did indeed refuse my offer of a meal, and compounded the insult by choosing a separate table.

It was as good a time as any to have my talk with Alexei, so when the dishes were cleared away, I ordered us each a beer and began my queries.

"What are you going to do now, Alexei?"

"I have not changed my plans, Ben. I may call you Ben?"

"Sure. Do you want me to put you in touch with American intelligence authorities? I have a friend high in the business who can make sure that you are well-treated and rewarded."

"You mistake my intentions, Ben. I am not a traitor, I do not wish to become a double agent, I do not seek asylum. I love the Russia that should be, but am disappointed at what she has become. I do not wish to return there at this time." I must have looked surprised, because he explained further.

"It is hard to explain how one can be a patriot and love one's country, but be ashamed of what her government has done to her people. And to the peoples of other countries."

He looked at me with an expression that begged me to understand. I found it difficult.

"Then, what do you want from all this?" I asked.

"I want not to be a part of what is happening to my country, I want not to carry guilt for some of the things I have seen and done, I want to be a coward and live somewhere that I can forget about labor camps, political purges, the disappearance of whole families because of an overheard disloyal remark. I want to find your Land of Oz, where everything is bright and beautiful, and leave behind memories of a drab, hungry nation where no one can be trusted."

"That's quite a speech for a KGB agent," I said. "Will you feel less guilty hiding somewhere, living the good life, and still knowing what's happening back home?"

"Probably not. But now I have no choice. When I saw all the money in that satchel, I acted like a Gushkov. With hardly a thought, I announced to Shelikov that I was leaving. Now, I will face immediate execution if I go back. There will be no discussion or excuses. I know—I have seen it with others."

"Do you have family in Russia?" I asked. "Wife, children?"

"None. If I had, I would not have even thought of doing this thing."

As I was puzzling over Alexei's complex set of loyalties and moral values, a small musical combo began setting up at the far end of the large central room. The local people moved from the dining area to the tables near the bandstand, and the waiters began serving beer to those who ordered. I remembered it was Saturday night, the traditional time for rural Alaskans to gather at the nearest roadhouse to dance, drink, or fight away the stresses of their work week.

I noticed Peggy Gibson moving with the others, but still taking a table by herself. I casually walked over to her.

"Can I buy you a beer in gratitude for your help today?"

"No, thanks. I'm just gonna have one, then leave."

"You driving back to your place tonight? That'll make a long tough day."

"I'll be OK. I'm staying with a girlfriend in Tok tonight."

I noticed that she had exchanged the bib overalls for a pair of reasonably fresh jeans. And the imprint of the pistol was no longer visible—although I doubt that she could have even slipped a calling card into that tight pocket, much less a weapon.

I moved to the table that Alexei and I had picked, ordered us a beer apiece, and waited with some curiosity for the music to begin. The combo was minimal, a guitar, violin (more probably called a fiddle), and a small, upright piano. All local talent judging by the friendly hails and joking repartee.

A sudden pang hit me as I was waiting for the band to warm up. In the excitement of the Russian invasion, the problem of the Red Starred Lady, the skirmishes on the river plain, and the murder of Sherry Jensen, I had not once been jabbed by the memory of Liz. But at this instant, when the thought emerged, the old pain struck, swift and sure.

Was it possible that my proximity to the sexy Peg had triggered a guilt reflex? I didn't think so—I had been very aware of the Amazon's nearness whenever it had occurred. She was hard to ignore, especially when beside me on a bouncy truck seat. But it seemed that her sexy, bigger-than-life perfection made her like an object of art, more to be admired than to be lusted after.

'Well, speak for yourself, Ben,' I thought. 'It's pretty obvious that that the male half of this room would like to admire her at very close range.'

The band tuned up and immediately jumped into Hank Williams mode. They weren't bad, the lead singer singing the classic Williams words in his own, rather good voice, rather than handing out a bad imitation of Hank. Then the combo slipped into some of the other country hits of the past few years, and a few couples stood to dance. It was a scene that could have taken place in any honky-tonk in Texas, except this crowd was noticeably less raucous.

I noted that Peg's foot couldn't seem to stop tapping time to the music, but when invited to dance by several of the local "prospectors", she politely turned them down. I thought of giving it a try myself, just for the sake of enjoying female company again, but I knew I was out of my league.

My dancing experience had, from a young age, been close and slow. During my youth, the only respectable way to get very close to a female body was while slow dancing. Jitter-bugging was OK if you were the athletic type, but I thought it left too much space between me and the object of my intentions. I had never picked up the knack of honky-tonk dancing, and didn't want the embarrassment of proving it to the crowd.

To my surprise, Alexei excused himself and approached Peg at her table. A few quiet words and they were soon cavorting with the best of the locals. Alexei definitely added life to the proceedings, his prancing reminiscent of some Russian folk dancing I had seen overseas. The male glances darted at him from the sidelines might have led to trouble, but Alexei Shilov saw none of them. He seemed as entranced by his partner as she by him. One bold local made a feeble attempt to cut in, but found himself frozen out. Alexei ignored him and Peg trod on his foot. The dance ended and the band took a break, as did Alexei, slightly limping as he made his way back to our table.

"You looked pretty good for a guy who got shot up this morning."

"I hurt more than is apparent," he said in his impeccable English. "One doesn't show pain in the presence of a lady."

"Hell, Alexei, she's seen the bullet holes. You're not fooling her."

"A matter of pride," he said stiffly, and eased himself into his chair. "She is a fine woman. Intelligent, beautiful, and she knows about growing wheat and barley."

"That's what you talked about? Half the guys in the room wanting to whisper love into her pretty ear, and you beat 'em out by discussing wheat?"

"I grew up in the Ukraine, and that is what we do there," he said. "She was interested."

CHAPTER 36

The Pursuit of Happiness

The Trooper Sergeant had been good enough to offer us a holding cell for the night, so Alexei and I hauled my sleeping gear over, threw the existing bedding into a corner, and sacked out on the stripped bunks. It had been the longest day I had put in for a long while and I was exhausted, tired, sore—and sleepless.

My mind rambled, halfway between sleep and wakefulness. 'You know that Nikki Gushkov is going to kill someone. Someone else. Why didn't you pull the trigger when you had him in your sights? Stupid ego, just wanting the satisfaction of seeing your booby trap work. Or, could you have pulled the trigger? Aside from war, have you ever deliberately shot another human being? Well, yes—up on the mountain at the Nike site. But that was to prevent a nuclear event that might have killed thousands. And you hadn't killed—only wounded the target. Not your fault though—you shot to kill.'

Somewhere between the beat of self-accusations and the pangs of conscience, I must have slipped into sleep. I was back at the bridge. I was in a steady prone position, the crosshairs on my scope were centered on Nikki's chest. He wouldn't kill anyone else. I put pressure on the trigger, determined to ease the shot off with no disturbance of aim, to terminate Nikki as a threat.

The trigger broke off in my hand. Nikki saw it and laughed. I tried to put the trigger back in place, but it was too late—I could hear the blue pickup truck approaching, could hear it stop, could hear a gentle voice question Nikki. Heard the pistol shots and

came upright in my bunk shouting "No, Godammit!"
 I was on the edge of the bunk, Alexei and the duty cop shaking me awake. It was dark, or as dark as it would get at that latitude on an August night. Probably about two or three AM, I thought. Maybe time for a few hours of sleep before the town woke up. I flopped back down and dropped immediately into a dreamless sleep that lasted until the Troopers came to work.

 Before we could get lined out toward breakfast, the Trooper's phone rang with a call for me from Jim McGann. I updated him on our situation, including the fact that Nikki was still on the loose, and that I planned to hang around Tok until that situation was corrected. I also mentioned that I was nearly broke, not having expected to need much money in a camp on the Gerstle River.
 "If you still need money," he said, "I guess Gushkov must have gotten away with it all. From what Shelikov said, there was enough money in that satchel to buy Tok. Speaking of Shelikov, we got him and his crew to Anchorage and they are probably leaving for DC tomorrow or the next day. The second Secretary to the Assistant Ambassador, or whatever he is, has been most complimentary about his dealings with you and your crew."
 "Did Mike and Neeta get back OK?" I asked.
 "Oh, yes. And Neeta's been hitting on me for the pay I owe you all for the contract job. I think she has plans to upgrade Mike's cabin, and I'm not sure he knows it yet. Should be fun to watch—from a safe distance."
 "And did you get what you expected from this contract?"
 "I did. Tell you more later."
 "Very good. I'm gonna stay up here for a while to look for Nikki. If I find he's gone south, I'll come south. Arrange with Sergeant Jordan about some money for us."
 I handed the phone back to the Trooper Sergeant and led Alexei over to the Tok Roadhouse for breakfast. I noticed he wasn't nearly as spry this morning as he had been while dancing last evening. Of course, there was less incentive this morning.
 As I finished mopping up my eggs with a huge slab of buttered toast, I eyed Alexei, who was pouring his second cup of hot, black coffee. I shoved my mug over toward him.
 "Me too, please." When he had obliged, I leaned back in sinful comfort, feeling that no one should want much more than a few

moments like this in his life. Except, perhaps, a clear conscience.

"Shilov, how do we get that sunnovabitch before he kills somebody else?"

"In my country, when we need to kill wolves, we use poison bait, or we use live bait and shoot them. But there is too much bait here, and we cannot be everywhere. You have a Sergeant and three or four Troopers watching a land as big as France.

"Nikki will steal food or whisky, or another vehicle, but how to know when or where?"

Sergeant Jordan entered and made himself at home at our table just as Alexei was finishing his comment. Jordan handed me an envelope with five one-hundred-dollar bills peeking out.

"Here's some walking around money. Your CIC buddy said there'd be a government check coming in to cover it. And we just got our first sighting of your boy. A liquor store just south of Tok had barely opened its doors this morning when a big bearded fellow came in, grabbed three or four bottles of Vodka, and took off. Owner said the guy waved a pistol at him, looked like he was going to shoot, then changed his mind and ran—with the owner's old white Dodge truck. Guy left him a used-up blue pickup with the gas gage knocking on empty."

"You have a plane to search from the air?"

"There's a volunteer pilot up now. A guy that happened to be in town on other business. He'll radio in if he sees anything that looks like a white truck. But if your boy just hunkers down under cover somewhere until night, we're helpless."

Alexei sat his coffee mug down with an attention-getting thump.

"I would like to ask a question," he said. On the assumption that his question might lead to some sort of solution to the Gushkov problem, we both listened.

"What is my status here?"

"Your status?" Jordan furrowed his brow. "What do you mean?"

"I came to this place as part of a diplomatic team working for the Soviet Ambassador. I abandoned my post for reasons which shame me, but I still carry a diplomatic passport and identification. I have broken no American law."

Jordan and I looked at each other, neither coming up with a ready reply.

"Am I a prisoner in custody, or am I at liberty to pursue my own interests?"

"I reckon you're free to pursue your own interests, as long as they are lawful," said Sergeant Jordan. "As far as I'm concerned, you're just another guy caught at the wrong place at the wrong time. Just don't screw up!"

"And as the closest thing here to a federal representative," I added, "I agree. At least, as long as she doesn't mind being pursued."

Alexei reddened and looked away; Jordan, now understanding the gist of the conversation grew stern for a few seconds, then smiled and relaxed.

"Whatever magic you used to thaw out our Peggy, you oughta' bottle it and sell it. The local boys would make you rich."

As the three of us walked back to the Detachment headquarters, I noticed that the younger men we passed seemed to defer to Alexei with respect; some with traces of awe. I even found myself wondering if he was privy to some secret Russian magic capable of bringing down a goddess.

CHAPTER 37

The Search

"May I have some money?"

Alexei stood before me embarrassed to have to ask; I was ashamed at his having to do so—I should have offered earlier. He was just as broke as I was.

I offered two of the hundred-dollar bills, then relented and offered three.

"You'll need more than I, since you're courting Peg. I can probably get more if I need." In fact, if I could ever catch up with Nikki, I planned to have a whole lot more. Alexei took the two hundred I first offered.

"Thank you," he said. "It will be repaid. Now, Peggy has invited me to see her farm, near the place called Delta. She must return to look after her stock, and she also wishes to visit the Jensen place and set things right there. I would like to go, and will return tomorrow to assist in finding Gushkov. If OK?"

"OK. But keep your eyes open. He doesn't know the country at all, and he could go gallivanting off in any direction on a whim. I'm beginning to wonder if he has a plan, or is just letting fate carry him wherever."

"If fate carries him to me, I will kill him— unless your law prohibits my doing so. I still carry my Tokarev." He reached into the pocket of his heavy field coat and produced the Russian issue service automatic that I had returned to him when we left the Gerstle. I had decided that he was an ally rather than an opponent—I hoped my guess was correct.

"I hope you're a better shot than he is," I commented. Alexei showed a slight smile and slipped the pistol back into its pocket.

Peggy Gibson showed up ten minutes later in her yellow GMC, and I last saw them driving westward at a brisk clip, Alexei behind the wheel.

I asked Jordan if there was a spare car or truck that I could use while the manhunt was on for Nikki Gushkov. It was a Sunday, but the state workers around Tok all knew each other and seemed not to stand on formality. After a few calls to some state Department of Transportation workers, he found a rather battered tan 1961 Ford F-100 stepside pickup that looked ready for the wrecking yard. It was unusual only in that it was a 4-wheel drive unit—few trucks of its generation were so equipped. A manual transmission, naturally, coupled to a two-speed transfer case with separate front-drive shifter. It would be a real bear to drive in rough terrain, but it beat the hell out of walking. The truck, it seemed, was up for disposal due to age and wear.

I thanked the Sergeant, filled the tank out of the Troopers' fueling station in back of the headquarters, and took it for a test drive. Shifting gears was a noisy procedure, accompanied by much clashing and grinding until I re-learned to match the speed of the engine to that of the wheels before jamming the gear lever into its notch. Trucks had come a long way in recent years, and I had nearly forgotten the techniques of double-clutching. The non-power steering needed a lot of muscle to horse the truck through corners, and the equally non-powered brakes required half my body weight on the pedal before any noticeable reduction of speed occurred. The clutch spring fought my left foot with vigor.

The Ford happily whined its way down the road at a dashing 45 miles per hour, complaining a bit when pushed to 55. There was a slight reek of gasoline in the cab, probably due to the fact that the tank was inside with me, tucked behind the seat. A fuel gage was hardly needed; the constant sloshing of gas on quick turns indicated (to a calibrated ear) the relative amount of gas remaining.

It had been a long time since I had driven a very basic truck, one which required the driver to integrate himself with the mechanics of the vehicle. It was plain I was going to have to actually drive this truck, and I was enjoying it very much.

I consulted a borrowed road map and steered a course for the liquor store that Nikki had visited this morning. It was a small log hut just south of Tok, and a local tow truck was about to haul the blue Jensen truck away for a thorough examination by crime scene experts. I stole a quick look before it left.

The bench seat and dash were still splattered with Sherry Jensen's blood, and an empty Russian pistol cartridge casing was rolling around on the floor. Nikki had made no attempt to clean the cab up or remove evidence. I hoped the forensic people would do a good job—I wanted absolute justification for what I hoped to do to Nikki Gushkov.

After watching the blue truck being towed away, I drove up to the shoulder of the highway and stopped, trying to put myself in the fugitive's shoes. Which way would he have turned? I suspected his journey would trend to the south, to the hope of buying passage on a plane or boat that would take him toward Mexico, toward his dream of booze, babes, and warm sun.

'Not that there's a helluvalot wrong with that.' I thought, envisioning what this local landscape would look like when winter came. 'But he's not getting there on the blood of Sherry Jensen if I can help it.'

I turned right and slowly drove southward, trying to see the country from the perspective of a greedy, hungry, and probably not-too-bright Russian fugitive.

A mile down the highway, I saw an old grown-up Jeep road leading off to the left. Heaving the old truck off the blacktop onto the trail seemed to revive her—she tucked her stiff 8-ply tires into the ruts and tracked on over the frost heaves like she knew what she was doing.

The trail was atop a long, low gravel ridge about 50 yards wide. The terrain adjoining the ridge was soft and swampy on both sides, veined with small sluggish streams, and unwelcoming to anything but a beaver colony. The reason for the existence of the Jeep trail became obvious at its end. About two miles from the highway, I faced a large, scooped out pond which had once been a gravel pit, probably used as a source for the built-up bed of the main highway.

I wrestled the Ford around with some effort and backtracked

to the highway, turning south again. I saw several other similar tracks leading to my left, out onto the wetlands, but assumed they would probably also end at gravel pits. Finally, a two-track led west, off the opposite side of the highway. There was no mailbox or other sign that it might lead to a dwelling, so it might be attractive to Nikki as a spot to lay up until dark.

I parked the Ford on the shoulder, just across the road from the turnoff, loaded my Winchester 338, and cautiously made my way along the track. The country on this side of the highway was wooded and the lane seemed to lead up into some low foothills. I walked about a mile into the woods, wondering if I would come upon an abandoned homestead or possibly an old mining claim.

What I actually came upon, as I rounded a sharp curve in the trail, was a big white Dodge pickup with a bearded hulk of a man standing in the bed pointing a double-barreled shotgun at me. Nikki was resting the gun on the top of the cab, the truck was headed outward, toward me, and I could see it wasn't going much farther—it had high-centered on a half-buried boulder which was now shiny-black with spilled oil from the ruptured crankcase.

CHAPTER 38

Bluffed

When Nikki recognized me, his face lit with a huge smile of satisfaction.

"I think I see you at bridge. Not sure. Now sure."

He raised the shotgun, making a show of cocking the hammers, one at a time. I mentally kicked myself. If I had seen that the shotgun wasn't cocked, I'd have had plenty of time to raise my rifle and fire.

"Where Shilov?"

I waved back over my shoulder.

"At my truck, waiting for me."

"Rifle down," he ordered, and I carefully put the 338 down, ensuring that the safety was OFF and the rifle ready to fire.

"Wait," he ordered. "Back from rifle."

I stepped back a few steps. He just stared at me. I stepped farther back. He grinned and climbed down from the truck bed. I watched as he opened the cab door and retrieved several bottles of vodka and a bag of jerky strips. One bottle was nearly empty. I could see that his face, arms, and chest had been peppered with bits of wood and steel from the burst rifle, but it didn't seem to bother him much. They must build them tough in Mother Russia.

He reached in again and slid out the satchel full (I hoped) of money. He jammed the bottles and the jerky into the satchel, looped a light rope through its handles and over his shoulder, and strode toward me, the shotgun ready. I took another step backward as he leaned over and picked up my rifle with his left hand. To my utter surprise, he then handed me the shotgun and began laughing uproariously, stamping his feet, and pointing at the shotgun.

Suddenly, I knew what the joke was. I broke open the shotgun and found myself staring into a pair of empty chambers. Whatever other faults Nikki Gushkov may have had; he possessed a robust sense of humor.

I feigned anger and loss of temper, whirled the shotgun around my head as though to heave it over into the woods— and flung it hard into Nikki's face. I was prepared to snatch my pocket pistol out and plant a bullet between Gushkov's eyes, but he was once again a step ahead of me. With a motion that was almost casual, he put out an arm, snatched the shotgun out of the air, and smacked me across the chest with the barrels.

"I don't want shoot," he said. "Shilov hear. But I kill you quiet, you make trouble."

His English was sketchy, but I found his meaning quite clear. I stepped back, rubbing the twenty-year-old scars that Gushkov's vicious blow had reawakened.

Satisfied that he had made his point, he handed me the empty shotgun and motioned me ahead. We began moving back along the way I had come, heading for the main road.

"Your American gun no damn good," he commented as we walked. "Bust when I shoot Shilov, you." He gestured toward his face and arms. "AK not bust; Mosin-Nagant not bust. Russian guns strong, not bust."

Nikki seemed in a mood to talk, although he kept his voice low as he did so.

"This gun bust too?" He tapped my Winchester. I chose not to answer, hoping this might make him uncertain, and somehow slow his reaction if he needed to use the rifle. He stopped, examined the rifle closely, and broke into a grin.

"Good gun. I see Winchester name. All Winchester good!"

He looked again, fingered the safety lever, and moved it back and forth. He then eased the bolt open far enough to see that the chamber was loaded, closed it.

"Which way safe?"

"Back." I answered, motioning toward the butt. I had left the rifle on "fire", thinking it might give me an advantage if I could seize it and turn it against him. Now, it seemed better to have it safe so that he wouldn't accidentally shoot me while playing with it. He made it safe and began to walk again.

I wondered what Nikki would do when we reached the truck and didn't find Alexei. He would have to assume that Alexei was in the vicinity—would he take the truck and flee, or would he set up an ambush for his ex-partner? If he chose to flee, he was unlikely to leave me alive. Should I jerk the little 38 out of my pocket and shoot him at the next opportunity? If he didn't go down at my first shot, the Winchester would rule the field—I would be unlikely to survive any kind of a body shot from 338 Magnum at close range.

But if I could escape into the bush, Nikki would have to assume there were two enemy to contend with. He'd be likely to try and grab the truck and run.

Apparently, Nikki's thoughts were paralleling mine; he stopped again and held out a hand.

"Truck key."

If I had another key of any kind, I'd have handed it over with apparent reluctance. Having only the real one, I handed it over with real reluctance.

"You walk ten meters front. See Shilov, wave hello."

I stepped out about 30 feet ahead and we continued our trek, Nikki alert and cautious, I, looking for just the right place to disappear into the bush without giving him a clear shot.

I rounded the last curve before the main road, and could see the front fenders of the old Ford, still where I had parked it. I continued another 30 feet so that it would come into Gushkov's view, then turned 45 degrees in the opposite direction and waved at an imaginary Alexei Shilov.

"Alexei! I'm back!"

Gushklov swung the rifle off in the direction I had waved, searching for his target; I dropped the shotgun and leaped over a ditch and into a thick growth of dwarfish black spruce on my right, running as quietly and low to the ground as I could. I angled forward toward the road, thinking that I might get one clear short-range shot if I could beat Gushkov to the truck.

I could hear Gushkov cursing as he realized he had been duped, but he was still unsure about Alexei and could take no chances plunging around in the brush with two antagonists to worry about. I made it to the main road in about ten seconds, took up a position that would allow a two-handed shot at Gushkov when he arrived at the Ford, and waited under cover.

The range would be about 40 yards—not difficult for a still target that didn't shoot back, but chancy for a running target that would instantly take advantage of a miss. I cocked the revolver and froze into a steady firing position. For ten long minutes, there was no sound, no movement.

CHAPTER 39

Gone Again

I had considered Nikki Gushkov an impetuous man with little patience, and had assumed that I could outlast him in the good old American Indian game of bushwhacking. Shelikov had warned me that one does not get to be a senior sergeant in the Russian army by being kind-hearted—I was now discovering that, while becoming unkind, he had also picked up a few tricks of woods-craft.

A peculiar whistling sound accompanied the flight of an object over my head. I looked up in time to see the barrels of the disassembled shotgun cartwheeling over and crashing into the brush behind. I jerked my attention back to my front, fully expecting to see Nikki in full charge toward me with rifle in one hand and pistol in the other. I saw nothing.

A very careful reexamination of the area around the truck revealed no obvious change. A slight flicker of motion beneath the high-sitting Ford caught my attention, and I fastened my gaze on the spot. No more movement for a half minute, then another flicker which resolved itself into the shape of a boot heel. The heel of a Russian jackboot, to be precise.

While I was distracted by the shotgun barrels, Nikki had evidently run from the cover of the woods beyond the truck and tucked himself up on the step just ahead of the driver's side fender. The boot moved up out of sight and the bottom of the satchel moved into view; the door swung open and Nikki rolled inside, slammed it, and started the engine. He ducked low, jammed the truck into gear against a screech of complaining steel, and accelerated south. I had time for two shots—the first through the right-side door, which probably didn't even penetrate the inner panel, and the second, more carefully aimed, through the rear window and very possibly adding to Nikki's superficial wounds.

The steady course of the truck told me that I hadn't hit any organ of consequence, so I helplessly stood and watched my quarry drive out of sight.

When I faced Sergeant Jordan that afternoon, having hitched a ride back to Tok, I instinctively stood at military attention and braced myself for a well-earned ass-chewing.

Jordan listened to my tale of ineptitude, made no offer to stand me at ease, walked around me twice, examined me like I was a shave-tail lieutenant, and shook his head doubtfully. Finally, he motioned me out of his office.

"Let's go over to the roadhouse. I'll buy you a drink—it's either that or throw you in a cell while I think things over."

I remained silent, not wanting to further incriminate myself. When the drinks came, we each sat without conversation, concentrating on the amber liquid. When it had disappeared and we had ordered another, he turned to me and spoke.

"Ben, to put your report in a nutshell, it reads like this." He took a deep breath.

"You took the state truck which I entrusted to you, and went man-hunting. You stumbled on the man you were hunting, letting him bluff you with an empty shotgun. Whereupon, you handed him a modern scope-sighted rifle, fully loaded, and set him loose with the state truck— which, I understand, was fully fueled with state gas. Then, for good measure, you shot two useless holes in said state truck as it departed for parts unknown."

"I think I might have worded that report a little differently," I said, "but in essence, you are correct."

Jordan fixed a harsh gaze on me and tried to hold it, but I could see a hint of a twinkle starting to show through.

"You know, Ben, the one good thing about your adventure is that it'll make any screw-ups I commit for the next month look petty. And I'm gonna tune the report for maximum laughs—out here in the boonies, we need all the entertainment we can get.

You might want to change your name temporarily, or go hide in Anchorage."

"No, Sergeant, I have other plans. The bastard's a killer, and he'll kill again if it suits his convenience. He's got my rifle, and he's got your truck."

'And he's got a couple hundred grand in cash.' I thought to myself, 'part of which belongs to me.' I had chosen not to mention the bag of cash, not wanting to have a trove of treasure hunters cluttering up the landscape while I hunted Gushkov down.

On the assumption that Gushkov would alternate driving, hiding out, and foraging, Jordan and I searched maps covering his probable course south. There were many side roads and trails that he could use for temporary lay-ups; covering or individually checking these areas was impossible with the resources available. And there was no way to guess at his rate of travel—Nikki might make all possible speed south, or he might kill a jug of vodka and sleep away the day on some out-of-the-way side road. The main route trending south was the Tok Cut-Off, which eventually merged with the Glenn and Richardson Highways, the first going to Anchorage and the second to Valdez.

Anchorage seemed the quickest way out of Alaska, especially for one to whom money was no object. A flight from Anchorage could put him down within easy distance of the southern border and Mexico.

Of course, Valdez was a seaport town—there was always a chance Gushkov could finagle (with the aid of cash) a berth on some south-bound vessel. Or, he could buy a plane ticket over to Anchorage and go south from there.

The only way for me to cover both was to plan an intercept in or north of Glennallen, where the highway split. Glennallen was around 140 miles from Tok, and the roads would barely allow a 40 miles-per-hour average on a straight through drive. Nikki could possibly be there by now, but I doubted he would take a chance on driving during daylight with aircraft obviously patrolling the main road.

"Sergeant Jordan, any chance you could get someone to fly me and my gear to Glennallen right quick? If I can beat Gushkov there and work with your Trooper Smith, we can block his chance at either Valdez or Anchorage."

"I already have Smitty setting up a checkpoint just north of Glennallen," he said, "but it's tough when none of the guys down there has ever seen Gushkov. If he changes vehicles he could steam through the checkpoint with little notice. There are a lotta' bearded guys in this state, and half the guys on the roads are wearing camo hunting gear.

"And," he anticipated my next comment, "if he grabs another car, he might have the ID of the late owner. You're probably right—you need to be down there just so we have someone who'll recognize him if he does bull on through."

Jordan made the arrangements quickly as I gathered my gear and waited to be driven out to an airstrip. I left a long-written message for Alexei, bummed some emergency rations from the Troopers' supply, and talked Jordan out of a handful of 38 Special Plus-P high-velocity jacketed hollow-point cartridges. These were about the most powerful cartridges available for 38 Special revolvers. They came with a warning that continuous use could damage standard revolvers due to the hot charges and high pressures involved.

I wasn't worried—I didn't intend to shoot but twice.

CHAPTER 40

Back in the Air

I was nervously awaiting the ride to the airstrip when I found that the airstrip was coming to me. The distant flutter of an idling Super Cub engine brought me out to the Trooper parking lot, and I watched a little Cub gliding along above the highway, drifting to a landing on the blacktop, and taxing off into the parking lot.

Jordan introduced me to the volunteer pilot and helped me load my gear into the skimpy space available. He instructed the pilot, a hefty middle-aged gentleman named Stripe, as to the probable location of the Glennallen checkpoint, shook hands with me, and stepped away from the plane.

I didn't know if Stripe was his first, last, or nickname, but he wasted no time. He did a perfunctory walk-around, made it a point to count the wings, grinning and waving two fingers at me as he did so, and fired up the Lycoming. When we taxied to the highway, he looked both ways, stuck his arm out in a parody of a left-turn signal, kicked the tail around with a blast of the throttle, and took us off eastward.

For a guy who didn't much care for buzzing around the state in small airplanes, I was certainly doing a lot of it lately. I uneasily wondered if adding hours in the air to my personal log was increasing the odds of disaster, or if it really didn't matter. There are those who say that when your "use by" date expires, the hammer will drop no matter where you are.

But I always favored the guy in the old joke who was asked if he would want to know the exact time he would die. He thought a moment, said "No, but I'd sure like to know where I'm gonna die." When asked why he'd prefer to know where, the guy replied, "So I can stay the hell away from there!"

I soon found that my pilot was the Joker in a stacked deck. He started a lively conversation centered around aircraft accidents and misadventures, moved on to tales of miners and trappers trapped by winter snows and forced into quite unbelievable acts to survive. Several times he would cut the engine and glide down quite close to treetops, then power-on and climb back to cruising altitude.

"Low on gas," he explained, "We get better mileage if we coast downhill once in a while."

It dawned on me that I had been introduced as a Federal Government person, and Stripe was indulging in the great Alaskan sport of "Spook the Fed". He probably assumed I was fresh from the bureaucratic halls of DC, and was determined to extract what fun he could from this boring trip. That was OK with me, as I was busy scanning the roads beneath, searching for anything that resembled a '61 Ford truck.

The searching was wasted time; I saw no tan truck, no bearded Russian striding south, nothing, in fact, to justify my even being here. Gushkov, of course, could have changed vehicles at any time, and could be driving any one of the cars and trucks headed south on the highway below. Or, he could have already passed through Glennallen and be streaking west on the fine straight highway toward Eureka.

I jerked Stripe's arm, interrupting a story about a Sasquatch-like creature rumored to roam the Iliamna country and prey upon those unwise or unlucky enough to be caught away from their camps at night.

"Can you make any kind of radio contact with Trooper Smith at the Glennallen checkpoint?"

"Maybe," he said, appearing somewhat miffed at being deflected from his story.

"Try," I said, and continued my search of the ground below.

Stripe fiddled around with the standard aircraft radio, then turned his attention to an obvious add-on that was screwed to one side of the cockpit. After a few minutes of exchanging call-signs and other mumblings that seemed to be intelligible only to the aviation world, he handed me a mike and his earphones.

"He's on."

I first made sure I was actually speaking to someone; I then passed on further information about the fugitive.

"He had a bushy beard, Smitty, but that could be gotten rid of pretty easily. He was dressed in camo-patterned hunting gear, like half the world out here, but was wearing black Russian jackboots. They should stand out.

"He could be driving anything; he has no compunction about killing anyone to take what he wants. One thing that might help—he had a rifle blow up in his hand yesterday, and has a multitude of small lacerations in his face, arms, and chest. Also, I shot out a truck window near his head—there are probably cuts from the splintered glass on the right side of his head and face."

There came a verbal explosion through the earphones followed by strange voices and much profanity.

"Get Stripe to cut straight for the Lake Louise intersection and set you down. The bastard buzzed through here about an hour ago! I'll chase."

Stripe hauled the Cub over on one wing and pointed it in what I hoped was a bee-line for the Lake Louise Road intersection with the Glenn Highway. We passed over low hills covered in dark spruce forest with few trails and no roads. As I looked down, I tried to imagine a traveler afoot in the midst of those dark trees.

With no sun to indicate north, one could wander for days hoping to break out onto a road or highway. And with only one north-south highway and one east-west, the odds were about 50-50 he'd strike out in the wrong direction and not return. This area west of Sourdough should generate excellent material for Stripe's Spook-the-Fed stories, but I noticed that he just looked down, grimaced, and kept his eye on the compass.

Smitty came back on the air, evidently speeding west out of Gennallen in an attempt to catch up to Gushkov before the Russian could find alternate ways with which to confuse us. He said that the man who drove through the Glennallen checkpoint was clean-shaven, had what appeared to be a skin condition involving his face and neck, and had a bandage of some sort wrapped around his head and jaw.

When asked his destination, he had mumbled about an infected tooth and pointed toward Anchorage. Smitty noted the official State DOT markings on the door of the truck and waved him on through. He had been wearing black jack-boots.

    I told Smitty that I was familiar with the vehicle, and that a steady 60 was about all she could do without the old straight-six engine coming apart. And that I'd try to block the road just before the intersection and hold Gushkov until Smitty came up and boxed him in.

CHAPTER 41

Road Block

Stripe jogged my shoulder and pointed ahead to the highway intersection we sought. I could see a dirt road leading at right angles to the highway and heading north, possibly a dozen or so miles, to a very respectable body of water.

"I'll land on the highway and pull off onto the Lake Louise Road. Then we'll spin her around and pull up to the intersection. When we spot him coming, I can pull out into the highway and block him."

I nodded and clung to the seat bottom while he demonstrated the fine art of converting a roadway into a landing strip. I noticed that there were no flamboyant hand signals as he expertly spun the Cub around and taxied to his chosen spot just north of the intersection.

"Stripe," I called as he chopped the throttle and let the engine windmill to a stop. "When we see him, why don't you start the engine again and get the prop revved up? I think he'd be damn' reluctant to drive head-on into that spinning meat slicer to doze us off the road."

"Sounds good," he said with a grin. "You're a little smarter than the average Fed. But what have you got for armament? You said this guy has a pistol and a 338 Winchester?"

"Well, I have a pistol too." I showed him the snub-nosed 38. "Do you have some sort of survival gun in this little buzz bomb?"

He reached back behind the seats and pulled out a battered old Stevens over-under 410 shotgun/22 rifle. Most of the varnish had been scraped off the stock by years of rattling around on the floor of the Cub, and the metal was largely worn brown rust. The barrel had been trimmed back to a length which would probably attract the interest of a Federal ATF officer.

"Sorry," he said, "but rabbits and grouse for the pot was all I was concerned about for survival. If I'd known I mighta' needed a people gun, I'd have brought something a little bigger."

"Well, load it up just in case. The 22 could slow him down, but a load of birdshot might distract him at the right moment."

We hauled the Cub around by hand and placed it so that a blast of the prop and hard left rudder should thrust it into position to block any traffic from Glennallen. I unlatched the cylinder of the snub-nose and positioned it so that two rounds of the hot-rod ammo would be the first fired. Fumbling around in the bottom of my pack, I found the small packet of mini-signal flares I usually carried there. I loaded two of these as the next to be fired, with the last hot 38 load as a final salute. The distress flares were pretty feeble, being sized down to fit a 38-cartridge case, but did burn with enough brilliance to attract attention if someone was seriously searching for you. Liz had insisted I add them to my gear as part of her ongoing campaign to prevent my untimely death by "stupid decisions and carelessness". She was never delicate when referring to my mountaineering skills.

A beep from behind the Cub reminded us that Sunday boaters and picnickers from the lake were beginning to wend their way home for the evening. An airplane parked on the road was apparently no novelty to them—three families drove around us, cut through the parking lot of a deserted looking country store, waved cheerfully, and set out for Anchorage.

Luckily, the location of the intersection provided a good view of any oncoming Glennallen traffic. With my 10 power Zeiss binoculars, I'd have no trouble identifying Gushkov long before he reached us. I had a chance to practice on several approaching cars and a pickup, all barreling west at high speed, wanting to get through the twisted roller coaster of road between the Matanuska Glacier and Palmer before dark.

The non-regulation radio in the Cub crackled and Smitty's strained voice came through.

"The bastard stopped at a gas station outside of Glennallen

and tanked up. Shot the owner twice and pistol-whipped his grand-kid. Headed your way. I'm probably five or ten minutes behind."

I re-cursed myself for not killing Gushkov when I could have, and saving two or three innocent lives.

'How many shots has he fired from that Russian service pistol?' I asked myself. 'Two at Sherry Jensen and two at the service station proprietor. The Tokarev has an eight-shot magazine, and I had not seen either Gushkov or Shilov carry any extra magazines. So, he has four or less rounds left, depending on who else he might have killed during his travels.'

Keeping that in mind, and that there were four rounds in my Winchester 338, Nikki Gushkov was quite capable of killing a lot more innocents if he were not stopped. I had already decided that he would be stopped—permanently if I could arrange it.

At the instant that I came to that decision, I saw the tan Ford pickup appear over a slight rise in the roadway and bear down on us like a charging buffalo. I yelled at Stripe, who immediately fired up the Cub and gunned it out into the roadway, spinning it into a precise left face and locking his brakes. As agreed, he kept the engine revving so that the spinning propeller would discourage any thought of ramming one's way through.

He got on the radio and alerted Trooper Smith, then carefully got out of the airplane, and seated himself on the left wheel, the Stevens 410 across his lap.

CHAPTER 42

A Taste of Hell

Gushkov obviously considered ramming his way through; light airplanes are pretty flimsy compared to old pickup trucks. When near enough to see the spinning prop blades, he braked hard. Realizing then that he couldn't stop the old Ford in time, he slewed it off the road and tried to power around the Cub and back onto the highway. Stripe and I had already checked out the ground on both sides of the road, and were ready for the next act. The truck struck the ditch, bounced several feet into the air, and slammed down in a low, boggy spot, sinking to its chassis. Nikki quickly tried reverse and every other gear available to him, only succeeding in spinning himself deeper.

Stripe reached through the window of the Cub, chopped the throttle, and resumed his seat on the tire, the 410/22 still in hand. I waited, pistol ready, for Nikki to decide on his next move. It didn't take long, and it was not what I expected—the driver's door flew open and Nikki emerged, charging across the 50 yards separating us, his pistol in one hand, my rifle in the other, and the money satchel hanging from his shoulder by a rope.

He somehow appeared smaller and less threatening without his usual bushy beard, but his technique certainly hadn't changed. He fired the pistol twice in his usual un-aimed manner, and with his usual lucky result. The acorn this time was the fat Super Cub tire on which Stripe was sitting; the resulting squeal of outbound air jolted Stripe's nerves to the point that the 410-shotgun barrel fired, peppering Gushkov's already damaged face

and shoulders with a fresh load of number-nine birdshot.
    At that range, the shot didn't penetrate deeply enough to do serious injury, but each individual pellet brought an immediately painful sting— unlike a bullet strike which often leaves a wound numb with shock, the pain coming minutes later. Gushkov emitted a roar which might have stopped a grizzly in mid-charge. He dropped the rifle and satchel, pawed at the pellet wounds, and retreated toward the still-open truck door at a dead run. He ran erratically, and I suspected he might have lost an eye to the birdshot.
    I lifted the small 38, took a careful two-hand hold, and fired a pair of shots through the open truck door; neither hit Gushkov, but both somehow sliced into the fuel tank behind the seat. The little gun bucked viciously under the recoil of the hopped-up ammunition and I could see the spray of suddenly liberated gasoline misting the inside the cab. As Gushkov pulled himself up onto the bench seat, he turned and emptied his pistol in my direction. I very deliberately fired the two flare cartridges into his chest.
    They didn't penetrate, of course, but they quite efficiently ignited the gasoline fumes which had suddenly filled the truck cab. In a matter of seconds, the entire interior of the cab was an inferno—Nikki Gushkov was scarcely visible, a twisting, burning shape among the flames which greedily devoured the cab and its contents. Gushkov's luck with random shots was still holding, however—I felt blood running down my left leg and into my boot.
    Nikki's screams died as quickly as he, his life having been abruptly sucked out of him by the searing heat. The punctured gas tank erupted with a billow of flame, the heat driving us back, our arms shielding our faces. I thought I could still hear Nikki minutes later, but realized I was hearing the siren of Trooper Smith's patrol car, which he had neglected to shut off while running over to check my injuries.
    Smitty and Stripe took turns rolling me around on the ground and checking for a wound, finally admitting that the grazing slice across my thigh was messy but not serious. The three of us manhandled Stripe's airplane back onto the side road and clear of traffic while a newly arrived Trooper shoo'd spectators homeward.

While we waited for Gushkov's tomb to cool, I updated Smith as best I could, Stripe filling in the details as needed.

"Stripe", I said, "thanks for that load of 410 shot. I think the bastard would've charged right through us if you hadn't peppered him."

"Hell, that was a luck shot, Ben. I had my finger on the trigger and when his bullet hit the tire, I thought I was shot—I just touched it off by reflex. As a matter of fact, when the air wheezed outta' that tire, I thought it was my death fart."

I had no comment to that, but I could see Smitty salting it away for a retelling around the Trooper Detachment tomorrow. If nothing else, we were furnishing fresh entertainment for the Troopers; I knew the story of my being bluffed by an empty shotgun and delivering a gassed-up vehicle and a scoped rifle to Gushkov would also be circulating tomorrow. Now, they had the "death fart" to discuss also.

Thinking of which, I retrieved my rifle and the satchel, which everyone had ignored while watching the old Ford burn itself out. Nikki was now a small, twisted lump of charred organic matter jammed under the melted steering wheel; I suspected it would take specialists to remove his remains in one piece, not that I cared one way or the other.

CHAPTER 43

Trial by Fire?

It was late when we finally got the Cub's tire repaired and made our plans for the morning. Trooper Smith offered us a holding cell in Glennallen for the night and assured me that the state would foot the bill for returning me to Tok in the morning, since Stripe was willing to fly me for the cost of fuel.

We dined at what Smitty assured me was the best restaurant in Glennallen. Afterward, I resolved never to relocate to that community

Later, Smitty joined us in the cozy holding cell that was to be our motel for the night. After he assured me that he was off-duty for the day, I dug into the satchel I had inherited from Nikki and extracted a bottle of reasonably good vodka. Smitty procured some glasses from the break room and I poured. It seemed to improve in quality as the level in the bottle went down, so our little party became more social than official as we chatted away into the evening.

"Ben," said Trooper Smith, "have you noticed that whenever you and I meet, shit happens?" Knowing what was coming, I put on my most innocent look.

"Why, Trooper Smith—whatever do you mean?"

He rolled his eyes and shook his head.

"First time I saw you, you were hanging upside down on your seat belt after somebody sabotaged the brakes on your truck. Second time, you stumbled into a murder victim up on Butte Creek during a caribou hunt. Third time, that hit man tried to whack you at the Eureka Roadhouse and you ended up watching him cartwheel off the Hurricane Gorge Bridge. Now, from what I can see, you're involved with the burning of a cargo plane, a helicopter, and a state DOT truck."

I carefully considered Smitty's allegations as I reached into the satchel and produced a second bottle of vodka. I replenished everyone's drink and pointed my pistol finger at Trooper Smith.

"You've got it backwards, Trooper Smith; did it ever occur to you that maybe you're the jinx?" I took another sip of the steadily improving vodka.

"You were there when my truck rolled. You gave me a lift across Butte Creek, and the next day I find a body. You were checking caribou tags at Eureka when I got the ketchup bath, and you had just made it to Hurricane when that gun moll shot the heel off my boot!

"Now, you get into the game here and suddenly we have bodies and burning vehicles all over the place. Yessir, I think you're the Jonah."

Leaving him to ponder the logic of my illogic, I climbed into the farthest bunk from the gathering, carefully taking the satchel with me, and dropped into a dream-free slumber.

After a really bad breakfast of runny eggs, half-cooked bacon, and lukewarm coffee at the "best place in town", Stripe took us off from the Glennallen airstrip and pointed the Super Cub toward Tok. We were in no rush, so cruised slowly and took time to appreciate the towering beauty of the mountains to the east.

Mounts Sanford, Drum, and Wrangell were individually visible in the distance, each with its own shades of color, and clothed in its own distinctive array of glaciers and ice falls. Even Stripe's endless stream of narrative faded away in the awe of such a view.

I felt a pang of sorrow that Liz was not here to share the moment with me. She used to avidly soak up such experiences, then relive them for us before a roaring winter fire or in the warmth of a shared bed. I mentally shook myself free of the thought and concentrated on the logistic and bureaucratic problems awaiting us at Tok.

Jim detached a set of earphones from a hook on the dash and silently passed them back to me. I put then on and waited.

Previously, most of our airborne communication had consisted of yelling back and forth between the front and rear seats. If difficulty in understanding arose, Stripe would back the throttle until we barely whispered through the air, and the point made in a normal voice.

Evidently, this was to be an important conversation since the ragged, smelly, and uncomfortable earphones were to be used.

"Ben, it was smart of you to load that little popgun with hot loads before our friend Nikki rode up."

I didn't respond.

"He seemed like a tough one—is he the guy that shot Sherry Jensen just to grab her truck?"

"Yep."

"And he had your rifle and shoulder bag, too. You musta' really been pissed off at him."

"Yep."

"And he shot the old man at the gas pump, pistol-whipped the kid for no reason."

"Looked that way."

"Well, the Troopers said the old guy'll make it OK. And the kid'll have a helluva bragging scar."

There was a half-minute of silence that I was reluctant to break.

"I noticed, Ben, that you left two signal flares in the cylinder when you loaded the Plus-P rounds. How come you didn't load her all the way with the hot ones?"

"Probably habit, Stripe. My girlfriend used to give me hell if I forgot any survival gear or signal equipment. I must'a just left 'em in out of habit. I was sorta shook-up with Gushkov barreling down on us and me with nothing but a handgun."

"You seemed pretty cool when you fired the first shots. Surprised you missed him and hit the tank. Next two shots with the flares, you caught him dead center. Damn flares tracked like tracer bullets."

I remained silent.

"Ben, you know a person might think..." I cut him off.

"Stripe, you know how rumors start out in this part of Alaska, half in fun, then evolve into myths that are told forever? Like my being bluffed with an empty gun and giving away the farm? Like your story of the Death Fart?"

I could see him nod his head. I continued.

"The last rumor or myth I ever want to hear would be one speculating that I deliberately set Gushkov up to be toasted, instead of just shooting him. Understand?"

He nodded again.

"Now, I'll concede that I figured he might fort-up inside the truck, and that it would take a fire to smoke him out before he killed somebody else. Maybe that's why I left the flares in the gun. But that's as far as we take this line of thought."

"Point taken," he replied, and never brought up the subject again.

CHAPTER 44

Who's in Charge, Here?

After a flashy landing on the highway at Tok, Stripe pivoted the Cub into the Trooper parking lot like he had a reserved space—maybe he did, for all I knew. These small outlying settlements were well insulated from the benefits of civilization, and many developed habits and customs designed to ease their own lives rather than to conform to townsmen's ideas of how things ought to be.

Sergeant Jordan and Alexei Shilov emerged from the headquarters building and met us in the yard. Shilov had ditched his camo hunting clothes somewhere and was garbed in brown canvas work pants and a checkered woolen shirt. His black jackboots remained, but were well hidden under his trouser legs. Judging from the fit of the clothing, I suspected that Alexei was slightly taller and possibly a little thinner than Peggy's former husband had been.

"I hear you got it done," said Jordan. "Congratulations are in order. Buy you dinner and drinks tonight if you promise to get the hell out of my district and not cause any more excitement."

"My own wishes exactly," I responded, "but I seem to have lost the transportation you so kindly provided. Any suggestions as to how to get Alexei and me back to Anchorage?"

"Before you do much planning, you should probably talk with Alexei for a bit." He walked back toward his office, taking Stripe along and leaving me alone with the Russian.

I had a pretty good idea what Alexei wanted to discuss, and a pretty good idea that I wouldn't be of much help. This would be a very personal problem and, hell, I couldn't solve my own personal problems. The thought of Liz flickered across my mind, and was hurriedly brushed aside.

"Ben, Margaret Gibson and I have found that we have many things in common, not the least of which is a love of farming. She has asked that I remain in Alaska, at her barley farm near Delta, and help her operate it. My knowledge of such farming as we did in Russia would add to her own." He awaited my reaction; I remained poker-faced.

"We have studied the matter carefully, and believe that the farm would easily support us during most years, would produce a surplus during good years, and probably lose money during bad years. This is as much as any farm of its size can be expected to do, unless as large as our collectives back in the Ukraine."

I refrained from comment, and he peered at me anxiously, like a young boy asking for the family car for a Saturday night dance.

"Alexei Shilov, what could I possibly do to help you in this matter? I can't give permission, not that you actually need it. And I can't guarantee that a KGB hit squad won't show up one day and kill both you and your lady. I can't say some American intelligence agent won't ferret you out and force you into active service against your mother country."

"And," I added, "at least one Alaska Trooper knows you're Russian."

"That may not matter as much as I had assumed," he said. "I have heard from Margaret that there is a small colony of Russian expatriates less than a hundred miles from here, and another located south of Anchorage. Apparently, a Russian accent draws very little notice in Alaska."

"I take it that a lot of your desire to live and work in Alaska has to do with your feelings for Margaret Gibson? Are her feelings the same?"

"Yes. And if it makes any difference, we plan to marry. And I should tell you, Ben, just to relieve your mind about some aspects of my defection. In anticipation of such an event as this, I long ago had a perfect set of American identification credentials made up." He smiled wryly.

"Many KGB agents do so in the event they fall from favor with the current regime. Most choose European nations or Great

Britain, but my embassy assignment persuaded me that the United States would be a better choice."

"It sounds as though things have really fallen in line for you, Alexei—or should I begin calling you by your new name?"

"You may shorten it to Alex," he said with a smile. "My new, but artificially aged papers prove that I am Alexander Tolson, born in Red Cloud, Minnesota. When we marry, Margaret will become Mrs. Tolson. Few of the local people know me, except as the stranger who stole Peggy Gibson away from them."

He said this last with a somewhat smug demeanor—one which courted disaster if displayed to the poorer losers among the local Peggy-prospectors. I just sighed and ignored it. If he wanted to enjoy the fruits of such a renowned conquest, he'd have to earn them on his own.

"It sounds like a plan that should work, Alex, if you don't get too careless or too cocky. And Mrs. Gibson is a strong woman—I'd suggest that you do most of the bending for a while. She was born and raised as an independent American woman, and she's been running that farm by herself for nine years. You'll find that she won't be as subservient as most of the women you are used to. Remember Neeta!"

His brow wrinkled in thought, and perhaps in puzzlement.

"Yes, I have noticed that Margaret seemed to bristle a bit at some of my comments and suggestions. I may have appeared somewhat authoritarian, but of course, someone must be in charge."

"It's her farm, don't forget. I'd recommend that you consider her in charge until she decides to concede specific responsibilities to you. American women don't necessarily want to be in charge, but they want a choice in the matter."

Having said a lot more than I had intended on that particular subject, I changed it.

CHAPTER 45

Citizen Tolson

"At least one American intelligence specialist now knows most of what occurred at our camp on the Gerstle River. Whether you have been identified as a KGB agent, I don't know. I don't think Shelikov would have any reason to tell him, but If he does find that a KGB agent is in the vicinity, he will do his best to capture him."

"I understand," said Alex. "I would have done the same to capture a CIA agent, were I aware of his existence."

I continued, "It's probable that all most people know is that there were two loose Russians making trouble in this area, and that one had a beard. Now, the people that witnessed Gushkov's death only know that a man, said to be Russian, was killed in a gunfight on the Glenn Highway. They will also know that he was clean shaven at the time."

I paused to allow Alex to absorb what I was saying, and what I didn't say.

"The Russian's body was burned far beyond any possibility of identification unless dental records become available, which I consider unlikely. So, if anyone were to try and determine which Russian died, he would find himself in a confusing situation."

Alex nodded, and I could see a flash of understanding across his face.

"If I adopt my new identity immediately, and begin a quiet life on the farm at Delta, I may never be connected with the two troublemaking Russians. Our embassy would certainly not spread information defamatory to Russia, and would be happy if the entire incident were to fade away."

I had noticed the luscious Margaret Gibson loitering nervously near the entry to the Trooper headquarters, obviously waiting to hear the results of my conversation with her newly declared fiancé.

"Why don't you go and talk with Peggy? I'll see you both at supper tonight."

I later discussed the situation with Sergeant Jordan, but in such a roundabout fashion that neither of us could be pinned with blame should the matter become official. I found it interesting that people trained in two different bureaucracies had learned the same tricks of evasion and non-commitment, and could come to a gentleman's agreement with the only evidence being a handshake.

I now anticipated that Alex and Peggy would have no trouble becoming respected members of the Tok, Dot Lake, Delta communities. As to who would be the ramrod on their grain ranch, I wouldn't have bet a nickel either way. Maybe I'd invite myself for a visit some day and find out.

A quick phone call caught Jim McGann still in his office on Fort Richardson.

"Hey, Buddy, I need to get home. How about sending a chauffeured limousine up here—preferably one with a built-in bar?"

"Hunnicutt, our agreement for paying you guys was a thousand a day each plus expenses, same as for the stolen warhead contract. Now, what with bush plane charters, equipment costs, Huey expenses for hauling people and gear, money for your bar bills at Tok, and whatever bills I get from the State Troopers, you're a money loser. I hear they may even bill me for the truck you set afire yesterday."

"Jim, it was all legitimate expenses. If you think about it, the lack of any one of the expenses you just mentioned, except maybe the limo, would have stopped me in my tracks."

"Well, your work's done now. You just get your ass home the cheapest way you can. I understand there's a bus service that can do the job. You can submit a voucher to me when you get back, and I'll reimburse you."

"Are you sure that's what you want, McGann?"

"Damn right. No more deluxe accommodations—you can cheap it out like the rest of us government peons."

"OK," I said. "I'll see you when I get back."

Jordan, Alex Tolson, Peggy, and I met at the Roadhouse for supper, Stripe having taken off for his home strip near McCarthy. The Sergeant signaled that he'd take care of the bill—no one objected and all ordered drinks.

While we waited, Peggy reached across and patted my arm.

"Thanks for taking care of Sherry's murderer—I couldn't have done it better myself."

"Not a pleasant job," I replied, "but it needed doing. And I wish I'd done it much sooner."

"You've been a soldier, I can tell. You must have killed before. Does that make it easier?"

"In the first place, never assume a soldier has killed people. Most military men can serve an entire career and never see an enemy.

"In the second place, killing on the battlefield is impersonal. The enemy doesn't want to be there any more than you do, but his job is to kill you. Your job is to kill him. There is seldom any hate involved. And no, it does not make killing on a personal basis any easier.

"And in the third place, how could you know that I had been a soldier?" She considered my question for a few moments before responding.

"A hard to define thing. Possibly a self-discipline not often found in today's men. Or a willingness to confront a problem rather than retreat from it. Perhaps, just a sense of duty." She laughed. "Or some indefinable combination of traits that triggers a woman's intuition. I just know I can usually pick up on a career soldier or law enforcement officer."

"Lady," I said, "I don't think I want to be around you much longer. I'll have no secrets left."

I turned to Alex. "You might keep that in mind, Alexander; this gal would make a good spy."

The meal was as good as plain fare can get, drinks were plentiful, and I found it hard to accept that I was unlikely to see these good people again. The loneliness of missing Liz had been partly filled by this group of diverse strangers I'd been thrown among, but the ache would return tomorrow.

CHAPTER 46

Bus Stop

The bus to Fairbanks was a twice-a-week affair, but luckily (for McGann) Tuesday was one of them. I picked a nice hotel in Fairbanks, collected all the newspapers I could find, and spent the evening soaking in a tub and catching up on the news of civilization.

Little had changed; both Anchorage and Fairbanks were booming with North Slope money, there were more ads for massage parlors than for merchandise, and ladies of the evening were still disappearing from the streets of Anchorage.

I was able to catch a bus for Anchorage leaving mid-morning, and thoroughly enjoyed watching the scenery while someone else did the driving. It was a slow trip, as the bus stopped at every settlement and at any place in between if flagged down by a potential customer. It was late in the evening when we saw the lights of Anchorage. From downtown, I caught a cab to Lake Hood and collected my truck.

Although I had only been gone about ten days, it seemed months. Plopping down in my own chair in my own living room seemed a sinful luxury, and tasting my own scotch added a touch of bliss. Now, if only Liz…

I mentally slapped my face and told my mind to find another subject. Compiling my list of expenses to present to Jim McGann seemed a good place to start. And I needed to check on Mike and Neeta in the morning. Plus, a call to Red Buckner to make sure we were square with him. I also wanted to call Trooper Smith at

Glennallen and thank him for his aid and support.

Hell, the after-action report to Jim would take all day, especially considering the careful massaging needed to keep Alex Tolson out of the picture. And, I realized, I was tired and not in the mood to any of the above.

I went to bed and knew nothing until the phone woke me at eight the next morning.

"Ben!" Jim McGann's voice cut through the remnants of my slumber. "It's Thursday morning. Where'n hell have you been?"

"Hey, McGann. How're you doing?"

"Mostly worrying about you. I haven't heard from you since Monday. What's happening?"

"Nothing much. Did what you told me and took the bus home. Got in last night. Figured to touch base with you today and start with the expense and after-action reports."

"You're saying it took you three damn days to get to Anchorage on a bus?"

"Well, Jim, it was Monday afternoon when you ordered me home the cheapest way, and that was by bus. Bus didn't come by until Tuesday, got me as far as Fairbanks. Bus for Anchorage left Wednesday morning, and got here late last evening. But don't worry—bus fare was really cheap compared to anything else."

I could almost hear Jim steaming when he realized what the order to "cheap it out" by bus was going to cost his department. At a thousand dollars a day, the extra two days would far outweigh the cost of an air ticket from Fairbanks to Anchorage.

"Get your ass to my office for a debriefing this afternoon." He slammed down the receiver.

When I had made my calls and assured myself that everyone else had made it back OK, I wrote up a list of expenses, charter bills, and equipment lost or stolen. I got a value on Mike Gearhart's blown-up Weatherby and added that to the total. Then I counted the days that each of us had been in the field, grinning a bit when I added my two days on the bus.

Also, I noted the destruction of one, each, truck, Ford, model 1961, suggesting that, since the vehicle was slated for disposal, the State of Alaska Department of Public Safety might consider writing it off.

I finally got around to what I had been thinking of all morning, the money satchel. I removed the various edibles and drinkables that cluttered the surface of the contents, and the dirty underwear that formed the second layer, all designed to discourage curious hands from prying deeper. Next, I extracted the grimy burlap bag that concealed the treasure trove.

I found myself staring at dozens of stacks of hundred-dollar bills—actually, 20 stacks, if Shelikov's count was correct. They were neatly banded with labels indicating $10,000 each, and with the logo of some overseas bank that I had never heard of.

I counted out three stacks of $50,000 each for the payment agreed upon for our rights to the Red Starred Lady and returned the $50,000 in "change" to the satchel to be forwarded to Dmitri Shelikov. Just in case the Russians might develop second thoughts concerning the deal, I hid our share in a concealed compartment in the stone fireplace of the patio on the bluff. I had found the hidden spot years ago after the original owner had used it to hide stolen gold. This was the first time I had found a personal use for it.

My debriefing by CIC agents was the high point of my day, not necessarily theirs. My story was pretty accurate to the point where Jim had airlifted me to the Gerstle River Bridge. Beyond that, even the exact truth would be confusing to anyone who wasn't there.

CIC agents were all called Mister; they wore no uniforms or rank. The relative ranks of those who questioned me was obvious from their attitudes. The first to question me was probably a captain or major, bucking for promotion and trying to look clever before the second. The second appeared bored and above this kind of thing. He would take hold and straighten everything out after number one had screwed it up. The major or colonel in charge, I guessed. The third was Jim McGann, who I guessed was a warrant officer. He would clean up after the others, and would rewrite the final report in such a way that nobody appeared too stupid.

CHAPTER 47

The Inquisition

"Yes, there were two Russian deserters.
"Yes, one had a beard."
"Yes, I think he shot the other one. No, I wasn't present at the time."
"I didn't actually see the killing of the Jensen woman, but assumed the bearded one did it."
"I'm pretty sure the bearded one stole the DOT truck, but didn't see his face at that exact moment."
"Yes, I heard a rumor somewhere that one of the Russians might be KGB."
"No, the person who was stopped by the roadblock didn't have a beard."
"Yes, he fired on my pilot and me, striking the airplane once and me once."
"Yes, I returned fire. I fired four times."
"How do I know? Because there was one cartridge remaining in my gun."

My last response may have sounded a little sarcastic, because number two stepped in.

"Mr. Hunnicutt, do you find this debriefing amusing?"
"No, Sir; it's definitely not funny."
"Well then, please confine your answers to specific facts."
"Yessir. I shot at the deceased four times. That was before he became deceased, of course."

"How many times did you hit him?"
"At least twice, I believe."
"You don't know for sure?"
"Sir, have you ever been in a fire-fight?"
"I ask the questions here, Hunnicutt—you just answer. Take over," he nodded to number one. "I'm gonna take a smoke." He retreated to his office.

Number one again took the lead.
"Do you think there may have been a third Russian?"
"Actually, there were seven to begin with."
"We only hauled out four on Mr. McGann's Huey. Where did the other go?
Is it possible that he followed the first two deserters?"
"Nossir. As explained in my written report, which you obviously haven't yet read, he died in the flames of Mr. Shelikov's chartered helicopter."
"Killed by the bearded Russian."
"No, killed while doing his duty in trying to save the plane."
"Let's see; the two deserters, Shelikov, and four other persons, one of whom may have been a KGB agent, that's eight—no, seven, plus the one who died, makes eight..."
Number one bogged down in confusion and looked helplessly at Jim McGann. Jim addressed the next question to me.
"How many were in the Tok area with you?"
"Two."
"What happened to them?"
"One was shot by the other, one was shot by me."
"Where are they now?"
"One is dead, probably in a freezer in Glennallen if they were able to separate him from the structure of the truck. The wounded one might be anywhere, or he might also be dead."
Number one, apparently regaining his balance, took over again.
"Where is the KGB agent?"
"If he was the clean shaven one we killed on the highway, he's dead. If he was the other one, maybe he's dead, maybe he's wounded, maybe he's back in Russia. If he was one of the other Russians, he's probably back in his embassy in D.C. I have seen no credentials, no ID, no badge, or document, that points to any

of the Russians as KGB. Who first said that there was a KGB agent among them?"

Number one fell silent, trying to collect his thoughts, and to recall if there ever was ever any proof showing that a KGB agent existed. I changed to another tack in an effort to completely screw up the routine of the interrogation.

"Jim, here's the left-over money from Shelikov's deal with my crew. Can you see that it gets to him—I don't want him to think we're thieves. Greedy Americans, maybe, but not thieves."

I handed him the $50,000 in cash while number one sat there bug-eyed. He immediately went in search of number two while Jim counted the packets and wrote me a receipt.

Number two abruptly returned, stared at the cash and, probably for lack of anything else to do, counted the bills again.

"$60,000," he announced. "Where did you get this?"

"From a Russian—and it's $50,000."

"I counted it myself, Hunnicutt. It's $60,000. Where did you get it?"

"Jim, please change this receipt to read $60,000. Sir, I got it from a Russian. If anyone gets around to reading my written report, it's all explained there. This money was in the hands of a deserter, and was recovered after his death. I'm returning it to Dmitri Shelikov, as it's the property of the government of the Soviet Union."

Jim made no move to change the amount on the receipt, knowing full well that number two had miscounted.

"Dammit, Hunnicutt," said number two, "we're getting nowhere here. Back to the KGB agent; where do you think he is?"

"Sir, I told you, I have seen no evidence whatsoever that any KGB agent existed. How could I speculate as to his location?"

"You were there during this entire cluster-fuck; you must have some idea where he might be."

"Sir, if such a person existed at all, and if by some strange act of transference, I became him, I'd probably haul ass for Russia. Wouldn't you?"

Number two stormed out, probably cloistering himself in his office for another cigarette. I didn't see him again.

Number one nervously paced the floor, started on several occasions to ask me another question, sputtered to a stop, and continued to pace. He had run out of sensible questions and obviously wanted to be gone, but wasn't sure that the boss would consider his task done. McGann merely sat, stacking and restacking the $50,000 in bills on the table before him.

Eventually, number one reluctantly said, "That'll be all." and left the office. Jim stood, shook hands, and said, "I'll see you in a day or two." and walked me to the main door. As I stepped outside, he stopped me with a hand on my arm.

"I'd advise that your crew doesn't spend any of that Russian money for a week or two. And your expense and daily logs look OK—I'll probably have your contract pay ready for you by next Monday.

"As to the Russian cash, I've got to warn you. The government will do its damndest to figure a legal reason to take it away from you. If it can't do that, it'll find some reason that you can't have it either. That's just the way things work."

CHAPTER 48

Shelter for the Night

It had been a long day of being questioned (more like interrogated) by the Intelligence people associated with Jim McGann and his organization. I came home sweaty and angry, half wishing I had never taken on the search for the Red Starred Lady, half wishing I was still out there on the Gerstle River flood plain where there was peace and quiet, and where the dangers were simple ones, easily understood.

Jim's people had gotten most of what they wanted, but were greedy for more. The capture of an ex-KGB agent would have meant a sure promotion in somebody's pocket, so the owners of the relevant pockets found it hard to accept that the rumored agent had evaporated from their grasp like a tundra ghost. When closely queried on the matter, I refused to speculate on unprovable intangibles. My only entertainment during the session had been watching the mounting frustration of my inquisitors.

It was a warm evening in early autumn, so I peeled down to jeans and T-shirt and went out to the patio on the bluff to enjoy a lengthy and spectacular sunset. It was spectacular enough while it lasted, but was cut short by the sudden intrusion of an ominous black cloud rolling in over the Chugach Range and down the Anchorage hillside. The accompanying rain accelerated from droplets to buckets in a matter of minutes, and the crack and flash of lightning, rare in Anchorage, added to the excitement.

A lightning strike on a promontory a quarter mile upslope

reminded me that my patio, with its iron grill and sheet-iron cook-top, was also an attractive target for lightning. I retreated to the house and contented myself by observing nature's tantrum through the sliding glass doors in the rear.

What little clothing I wore was soaked, but I decided to let it dry in place while I watched the storm blow itself out.

Just after full dark, I thought I heard a light knock at the front door. It was what I called, the 'Girl Scout' knock, light but firm. Wondering who the hell was dumb enough to be stumbling about in such a storm, I took the little 38 snub-nose from the mantle, slipped it into my pocket, and went to the door.

When the door swung wide, I stood transfixed, sure that I was hallucinating due to some nearby lighting strike.

Liz, my Liz, stood before me, the pouring rain streaming from her in cataracts, her hair hanging limply around a face bare of makeup, her clothing soaked and clinging like moss to a tree.

I stepped forward, took her small overnight bag, and wordlessly led her back to the bath area. I carefully removed her soaked clothing, one piece at a time. I took a fresh towel from the linen closet and patted her dry, working as delicately and gently as though she were made of finest lace.

She took my hand and led me to the bedroom, and to this morning's rumpled, unmade bed. We slowly and quietly reacquainted ourselves with each other, remembering and exploring at an unhurried pace.

Our final coming together was not in a flood of pent-up passion, but rather as a tender offering, a gentle loving acceptance, and a mutually grateful exchange of intimacies and caresses. We lay entwined for hours, still in silence, questions, and answers unimportant, basking in closeness and togetherness.

I finally dozed, waking in the early morning hours alone in my bed. I began reviewing the night in my mind, trying to convince myself that Liz was real—that she was here and not some erotic dream summoned from a night of thunder, lightning, and witchcraft.

A clatter from the kitchen removed all doubts.

I quietly left the bedroom and peered around the corner into the kitchen. Liz, as fresh and cheerful as ever, was setting out my eggs and toast. As soon as she heard the shower stop, she would put them to heat; when I arrived in the kitchen, they would be waiting, four eggs over hard, golden toast with too much butter, and coffee steaming away on the stove.

I headed for the shower, and when I sat down at the kitchen table ten minutes later, all was as I had foretold. Liz assembled her cereal and fruit and we ate in silence. Neither had uttered a coherent word since her arrival, and neither wished to spoil the magic of that quiet, intense night. I glanced out the patio doors at a landscape washed fresh and clean by the night's storm, looked back at Liz, and thanked the world for being perfect.

Finally, over coffee, we seemed to agree that talk was needed.

"Where did you get that last one?" she asked.

"Last what?"

"Last bullet wound."

"How...?" I began.

"Dummy! I mapped every square inch of your stupid hide last night. There's a bullet graze on your left thigh that wasn't there on my last survey."

This led to a lengthy description of the Red Star affair which, including her cross examination on the subject, lasted nearly all morning. I'm not sure how much of the tale she believed—she knew I wouldn't lie to her, but she also knew that I didn't always reveal things that she didn't need to know.

At least one part of my story was verified early in the afternoon when a truck pulled up in my driveway and a deliveryman rapped on the door.

"Mr. Ben Hunnicutt?" I nodded.

"Got three crates for you. Looks like they came from overseas. Sign here."

A little puzzled, and wondering if I should call the bomb squad, I dragged then into the entryway. As the truck backed out to Rabbit Creek Road, I examined the crates. From Russia, plastered with all sorts of labels, certifications, and diplomatic warnings, one was addressed to me, the other two to Mike and Neeta in care of me. I laughed with pleasure—Dmitri Shelikov was true to his word. I was willing to bet these were three crates of Ambassadorial Grade Vodka, pledged as replacements for the bourbon that had been pilfered from our camp.

I retold and enlarged upon the incident, which had been only a footnote in my morning's story to Liz. On opening the top of the crate addressed to me, I discovered a very ornate envelope with an embassy seal of some kind impressed in wax. The enclosed letter was hand written in old fashioned script. I read it, thought for a moment, and burst out in uncontrollable laughter. Now I knew why Shelikov had made his final comment as I was preparing to hunt down the two deserters: "The money in that bag may not be worth risking your life for."

Liz seemed baffled at my reaction, so I handed the letter to her. She read aloud:

My dear Mister Hunnicutt,

It is with pleasure that I keep my promise to replace the whisky purloined by my unruly crewmen. This Vodka is the finest available, and is usually reserved for Ambassadorial Dinners. I hope you and your friends enjoy it.

Perhaps it will atone for the matter of the cash, which I will assume you have recovered. I wonder, do my two deserters still live? I do not expect you to answer that question.

I can explain the counterfeit cash subterfuge best by stating that the Soviet Union is not in the habit of paying for property to which it already holds title.

Your Obedient Servant,

Dmitri Shelikov
2nd Secretary to the Assistant Soviet Ambassador to the United States
Washington, DC USA

CHAPTER 49

Profiling 101

When I finally stopped laughing over the scam that Shelikov had pulled on us, I lit a fire in the fireplace and we lay before it while Liz told me her side of our year apart.

"I finished the course in Human Sciences last month—first in my class, I might add." I rewarded her with a kiss on the nose.

"We were finding out from earlier students, profilers, we called ourselves, that our system actually worked if conditions were right. We couldn't zero in on a killer in a crowd, of course, but if a group of suspects had been identified, we could often pick out the one or ones most likely to be involved. More often than not, later close scrutiny of the suspects led to evidence of their guilt."

I was a little dubious, but since I wasn't in the police business, I wasn't in a position to criticize. But I had to needle her a little bit for old times' sake.

"So it has to be someone the police already have an interest in. Suppose you tell them to look for someone who hates his mother, has an inferiority complex, took dancing lessons as a kid, and was afraid of heights. And suppose one of the persons of interest meets those specs so you finger him to the cops. They arrest him. But he didn't do it."

"No—they don't arrest him. They just watch him closely. They couldn't make an arrest without some proof of guilt. Probable cause and all that kinda' stuff, you know? And he could be innocent—in any city there are probably scores of poor souls who match those criteria, but maybe only one who went over the line."

"And I'll bet you're here in connection with that series of street girl murders that have been plaguing Anchorage for the past year?"

"Yes," she said, "I'm doing a sort of field study of this series of kills to check our theories against the real world. Call it graduate studies. I'll work with the Anchorage police to learn all I can about the murders, apply the Bureau's profiling techniques, then follow the investigation and see if the killer, when he's caught, fits the pattern."

"So, your stay is indefinite?"

"I stay until the case is closed, one way or the other, or I'm called back."

"Can you stay here with me?" I was sure her answer would be no, considering how the FBI stigmatized mixing business with pleasure.

"I'm attached to the APD now, not the local FBI office. I'm expected to rent a room somewhere and work with the locals until the show's over."

"The rent here would be quite reasonable," I said. "I'm sure you could afford it."

"Thank you, Mr. Landlord; I was hoping you'd ask. Now, since I came by taxi last night, I have to go to the GSA motor pool and pick up a car. Don't drink up all the vodka while I'm gone."

I gave Liz a ride to the government motor pool, then headed out to Eagle River for a visit to Mike and Neeta. Someone had to tell them about the counterfeit payoff before they mentally spent it. I didn't see any new fripperies around the cabin, so figured we were OK for a while.

I waited until our first cups of coffee had gone down before I brought up the subject of our pay for the expedition.

"McGann said he expected our pay for the government contract to be ready Monday. If you two want to come over to my place for the day, I'll get him to deliver the checks there. As for the Russian payment... oops, I gotta make a quick call." I excused myself and dialed Jim McGann's office on Mike's old rotary phone.

"Jim. Ben here. When you come over to my place Monday to

deliver the checks, bring the 50 "K" I left with you yesterday. And best you don't show it to your bosses until later—we're gonna have some fun with it. Get here about two if you can arrange it."

After hanging up, I explained to my partners how the Russian had scammed us—that the money was probably counterfeit. I showed them the letter from Shelikov and watched their faces as they slowly absorbed the meaning behind his words. At first I saw anger, then amusement and open laughter. I was glad they saw it my way. After all, we had tried to extort Shelikov into paying an exorbitant amount of money for something to which we had no legal claim, and which had no particular value as it sat. My harping on salvage rights was a ploy I had pulled out of the air, hoping that Shelikov didn't know any more about the laws of salvage than I did.

His actions regarding the vodka were more than generous, however—at least, assuming that the fancy bottles weren't filled with water. My partners promised to show up shortly after noon to collect their pay and their loot; I promised to have one bottle out and ready for sampling.

I arrived at my place just before Liz showed up in a typical plain-Jane government sedan. I told her of my visit to Mike's, and of having them here Monday when McGann showed up with our checks. I was working on a plan to use the counterfeit money to extract some kind of extra benefits from the Army CIC. Not so much from greed, but to embarrass the snotty number two who had gotten in my face yesterday.

Liz had dropped by the Anchorage Police Department and the Alaska State Trooper offices on her way home, and had been pleased with her assigned counterparts in both places. She had expected the usual resentment of the FBI that often mars such partnerships. She suspected both agencies were feeling a touch of guilt that the killings had not been recognized as probably serial until late in the game.

Women had died who might have been saved if the investigation had begun sooner.

CHAPTER 50

Reliving Old Times

That night, we made no attempt to renew last night's lovemaking, but lay contentedly in each other's arms with only the occasional kiss or caress between periods of sleep.

In the morning I quietly eased out of bed, dressed in the bath, and prepared breakfast for both of us. A few minutes before it was ready, I woke Liz by wafting a fresh cup of coffee a few inches in front of her face and holding the saucer while she sipped herself into wakefulness.

Over breakfast, we discussed the possibilities of the weekend. Neither of us having any claim on our time until Monday, it seemed like a good time retrace some of our earlier explorations, to rekindle old memories of our first taste of Alaska. I threw the bare necessities into the home-built camper in the bed of my truck, and we launched ourselves onto a destination-unknown trip south to the Kenai Peninsula.

We popped in for a quick look at Portage Glacier, the scene of a shoot-out and chase that had led to the first realization of our mutual love. During the years since that escapade, the face of the glacier had receded a good quarter-mile. At this rate, another ten years would find it hiding around the curve of the mountain, invisible from the traditional viewing area.

An hour from the glacier, on a momentary whim, I steered onto the Hope road and we slowly enjoyed the winding way to the barely existing settlement of Hope. A store, a restaurant, and a handful of tourists were there to greet us, all unchanged since our last visit five years ago. The town site was almost a tidal mudflat and was located on the south side of Turnagain Arm. One could easily see the traffic across the Arm on the Seward Highway, mostly following in our earlier footsteps.

I looped around and reconnected with the Hope road, stopping near the bridge over Resurrection Creek. We got out and watched the salmon struggle upstream from the arm toward the spawning grounds in the valley.

Fishing season was in, and I had a license, but I had brought no fishing gear along. Cautioning Liz to keep an eye out for tourists or Fish and Game enforcers, I descended to the stream beneath the bridge, picked out a large male still bright from the sea, scooped him out of the shallow water, and tossed him into the bed of the pickup.

We drove to the Palmer Creek Valley road and turned south up the spruce-covered grade. The sight of a small flock of spruce grouse pecking away at the road gravel almost made me wish I had forgone the salmon for rich dark grouse breast, but no use being greedy. At the top of the grade, where the road broke into the open, there was a clearing with a panoramic view of a large north-south valley with the remnants of old gold mines scattered along the east and south wall. We parked and cleared a space for a small fire. Liz scrounged some firewood while I cleaned and fileted the fish. I put a healthy (or un-healthy?) glob of bacon grease in a pan, dropped in the filets, and sprinkled them with a generous coating of cornmeal.

With fresh-caught salmon, this simple preparation, and immediate cooking to a golden tan over an open fire, cannot be beaten for delicate flavor and just-right crispness. I believe the only reason Liz puts up with my occasional illicit poaching of a salmon is her love for the illicit results. Anyhow, she has yet to turn me in.

Resisting the urge for a nap, we left Palmer creek and motored back to the Seward Highway. I hung a right and headed us toward Seward at a lazy clip, stopping once in a while at an especially nice viewpoint. I showed Liz the trail leading up to a Falls Creek gold claim named the Katy Bee that I had checked out while chasing stolen Vietnamese gold—the claim that had given a doggedly tenacious miner the nick-name, "Hard Luck Stan".

We rolled into Seward in late afternoon; I wanted to visit the

Brandt family again so that Liz could renew acquaintances, but we decided to wait. We knew that a visit right now would result in an invitation to their evening meal, and it was unlikely that they would be prepared for two guests.

We camped on the beach near the ferry terminal and took our meal in a local restaurant. When we thought the Brandts would have finished their meal, we walked up to Second Street and on to the Brandt home. I knocked and the door was opened by son Jody, who appeared in my eyes to have grown a foot since my visit the previous summer. Nina, Gary, and Jody seemed equally happy to invite us in.

Jody took immediate possession of Liz, Nina built a pot of fresh coffee, and Gary magically produced a bottle of bourbon. Liz was a surprise to them all, as I had explained during my last visit that she might be gone for good. I let her take care of the explanations; Gary and I clinked glasses and exchanged meaningless man-talk.

Liz and I walked hand in hand back to our campsite on the beach. I built a small social fire for us to stare into as the evening passed. The conversation strayed from one subject to another, none important enough to linger over. Later, as we settled into our sleeping bags for the night, I thought about this golden day. There was, in truth, nothing special about it. Brief visits to places we had visited many times before. Scenery we had viewed before. A warm reunion with old friends and a campfire on a starlit beach.

But six months ago, deep in the depression of losing Liz, I would willingly have paid almost any price to again live such a day.

'Value what you have while you have it, Hunnicutt,' I told myself. 'You don't know the real worth of anything until it's gone.'

CHAPTER 51

Magnum

We made a leisurely drive north, admiring the turquoise waters of Kenai Lake, and turned off to Cooper Landing. Gwin's Lodge furnished its usual good coffee and excellent dutch-apple pie. On seeing me come in the door, Gwin cut a slice without an order; Liz glanced at my generous slab and pulled it over in front of her. Gwin grinned and cut me another.

After a little heavier lunch than we needed, I drove on across the bridge and turned into Bill Fuller's gun shop and shooting range. A couple of familiar faces were hovering over the shooting bench, so I guessed that a new rifle was being evaluated and drifted over to get in on the excitement. Liz went to the house to pay her respects to Betty Fuller.

The rifle turned out to be a replica of a Hawken mountain rifle that Bill had just completed. A half-stocked muzzle loader in 54 caliber, Bill had finished it more ornately than usual. He had fitted it with a fancy pewter nose cap and had set a brass patchbox with a fancy lid into the right side of the buttstock. The wood grain was more elaborate than the usual plain grain used on mountain rifles. All in all, a handsome rifle without being overdone.

Original rifles as preferred by the early mountain men were sturdy, heavy rifles that could stand falling off a horse or being used as clubs without damage. Mountain men considered anything fancy as useless foofaraw unless it could be traded for fur or a squaw.

"Does it shoot as good as it looks?" I asked.

"Don't know," was Bill's answer. "Haven't got around to shooting it yet."

Liz appeared about that time, and was greeted enthusiastically. A woman who could shoot was always welcome on the range; a woman who could shoot well and was a looker was doubly welcome. Liz qualified on all counts.

"Hey, Bill, I need to knock the dust out of my service pistol. OK if I set up a target and let off a few?"

"Sure! Mike, why don't you..." Before he could finish, Mike and a helper were trotting down range with targets and a staple gun.

"25 yards?" Mike asked over his shoulder.

"Make it 50," she answered, walking over to my truck to get her shoulder bag. When Mike and his assistant had returned and the range was clear, she slipped her Smith & Wesson Combat Magnum out of its special recess in her bag.

Opening the cylinder, she dumped the cartridges, checked the bore for obstructions, and reloaded. We all donned ear protection and stood by.

The spectators were entranced by the little powerhouse of a pistol. Liz had won it in an FBI competition years ago, and it was a bit non-standard. The caliber was 357 Magnum, the barrel 4 inches long, and the butt specially modified to a rounded configuration. The rounded butt allowed a better fit for small hands, and was less apt to snag when slipped out of the special recess in a lady agent's shoulder bag.

I had once mentioned to her that a rounded butt felt better in my hands also, but received only a scathing look.

"Clear to fire?" she asked. When cleared, she took the standard one-handed slow-fire position and squeezed off six deliberate shots at the first bull. As soon as she had cleared and benched her weapon, one of the watchers retrieved the target. It showed a nice cluster of holes that could be spanned by a large hand. Proficient shooting by any standards with full house magnum loads.

"Decent shooting," commented a young man whom I hadn't met, "but probably a little slow if your target's shooting back."

"You're right," said Liz. "If the target's shooting back, I do it this way."

She speed-loaded, dropped into a combat stance with a two-handed hold, and snapped off six fast shots at the second target.

She looked over at the man who had made the comment.

"You wanna fetch that target for me, son?"

He blinked, looked uncertain as to whether it would be manly to obey her. The rest of us awarded him a stony stare until he trotted down range and returned with the freshly perforated target. He spread it on the bench revealing a well-centered group that could be covered by a closed fist.

After undergoing a shower of congratulations, Liz went into the shop to clean and re-secure her weapon; her critic climbed into a dirty red Ford pickup and left the range. When I asked who the guy was, the answer was embellished with laughter and rude comments.

"I hate to tell you," said Mike Lineman, "but that's the newest addition to the Soldatna Police Department. I doubt we'll see him here again until he's done a lot of practicing."

Having had the privilege of watching Liz impress the hell out of a bunch of seasoned shooters, I felt that my day was complete and signaled Liz that I was ready to head home. I went into the house to pay my respects to Betty; when I emerged, Liz was aboard and ready to travel. I waved a goodbye to the group and we set out for Anchorage. Liz was quietly smug about her showing on the range, and I was proud for her. Such moments are rare when you're a woman in a man's world.

Instead of being tired from our two-day road trip, we felt oddly refreshed and ready for the coming week. We had made a casual visit into the past, ignoring thoughts or conversation about Anchorage's crime problems, my coming conflict with the CIC, and any concerns about Shilov's sly double-dealing. Our minds and our souls were well rested and ready for action.

CHAPTER 52

To Dmitri

Mike and Neeta showed up after lunch on Monday. The weather was pleasant so we all gathered at the stone patio on the bluff, soaking up sun and watching the distant mountains change color. Neeta entertained Liz with her own unique version of our adventures with the Red Starred Lady—which, I had to admit, were more colorful than my own dry account.

"When Jim gets here," I reminded everyone, "don't let slip that the stash of cash may be counterfeit. He doesn't know yet, unless he had a bill checked. If we can put something over on the bureaucrats, I don't want him to be collateral damage."

"I may not be able to stay for the show," said Liz. "I have to meet my APD contact at three when he comes on shift."

About 2:30 we heard the crunch of tires on gravel and Jim McGann showed up in his own private vehicle. I waved him down to the bluff and offered him the least rickety of the unused lawn chairs. He shook hands with Liz, saying how good it was to see her again, asking no questions as to her business here.

"First, let me deal out the payroll," he said. "Your expenses were all approved, and the basic thousand bucks a day for your time. Ben hung around Tok and Glennallen a little longer than I expected, but the bosses thought the results justified the extra days." He handed government checks to the three of us.

He turned to me. "They finally got around to reading your report," he said, "and they're still trying to count Russians. Wondering about the rumored missing KGB agent."

"Well," I said, "if they want, I'll go back to the Gerstle River and hunt for the guy—for a thousand a day."

"I reckon you would," Jim replied. "But speaking of thousands of dollars, the brass is unhappy that you guys collected so much from that guy Shelikov, and for something you didn't even own. They feel that the deal was shaky and the entire two hundred thousand should be turned over to the government."

"You mean, in the sense of fairness, we should return it to the Soviet government? I guess I can see their point—it would certainly help international relations."

"Oh, no, no. They mean it should be turned over to our government. Any money obtained through questionable means may be thrown into the operating funds of the agency that acquires it."

"And they would love to have another 200 G to play with? Jim, how do they justify that in their little cob-webbed minds?" I hauled the original Russian money satchel from under my chair and scrabbled through its contents.

"See, Jim, here are copies of the quit-claim documents we agreed to. You'll note that they do not say that we claimed the C-47 as our property. They state that we waive all rights to the plane and concede that it is Soviet property to do with as they see fit."

He scanned the papers and returned them, looking a bit puzzled.

"And they were willing to pay you 50 grand apiece for this agreement?"

"Here it is." I picked up the satchel and shook it. "That we were willing to send the left-over 50 K back to the Russians should prove that we made a good-faith bargain."

Poor Jim sat with his head in his hands, obviously trying to extract some logic from the claims, counterclaims, and orders from above that pressed down upon him.

"Look, I've got to take this whole mess to my bosses and see how they want to sort it out. Here's the left-over 50 K. Put it with the rest and wait until I get back to you."

"Who decides?" I asked. "That obnoxious guy that kept retreating to his office when three syllable words were being used?"

"Yeah, he's the light colonel in charge. Got promoted past his capabilities when he made first lieutenant."

"Look, Jim, we don't want to screw up the entire CIC. And we'd probably admit, after a few drinks, that the 50 grand apiece was largely unearned." I stopped short.

"Speaking of drinks, we have here," I pointed to an opened vodka bottle and glasses waiting on the cooktop, "a gift from the distinguished Dmitri Shelikov in repayment for some of our whisky that his men stole. I suggest that we sample it in the name of international relations." Waiting a full second and hearing no objections, Liz and I poured a few fingers in each glass and handed them out.

"For those of you who may now be in a duty status," I commented, "I understand that vodka does not linger on the breath if taken in moderation. To Dmitri!"

The vodka lived up to its reputation, as confirmed by surprised smiles on five faces. The two who were on duty refused refills, but we Red Star hunters didn't hesitate to try seconds, just to confirm our first impression.

"Jim, I don't know what might placate your bosses in regard to the money. I feel that we are legally OK, but the last thing we want to do is to get into a prolonged hassle with the Army or the government. In any drawn-out dispute, the government wins by sheer patience and manpower. They'll spend a million dollars to retrieve a hundred thousand, just on general principles."

"You're right, Ben. And this boss we have will be even harder to deal with because he doesn't like you. Your question during the interview about his ever being in a fire fight? You couldn't have hit a more tender spot if you tried."

"Well, do what you can for us, Jim. We might be willing to accept some sort of bonus for a job well done. We were under hostile threat, you know, and there were shots fired. Plus, we got the briefcase for you. Or for him.

"A reasonable bonus, free and clear of bureaucratic entanglements, and my partners may just hand him the satchel as is, where is."

"I'll talk to you tomorrow, Ben. And I'll give you the details on the briefcase then. You'll be home around noon?"

CHAPTER 53

One Suspect, or Many?

Jim took his leave, as did Liz, allowing us Red Star partners to relax, relive our adventure, and concentrate on the benefits of fine vodka. For the first time, I described in detail the events occurring at the Gerstle River Bridge and afterward. I did withhold the final disposition of Alexei Shilov and his transformation into Alexander Tolson. And though I was reasonably forthright about the demise of Nikolay Gushkov at the Lake Louise intersection, I was still struggling with my own truth about that matter.

"Ben," asked Mike, "what do you think you can get outta the Army in exchange for the Russian money? And what's gonna happen when they find out it's queer? We might be getting into more trouble than it's worth in the long haul."

"I'm gonna tread softly, Mike, until I get some idea how far they'll go. If they'll throw in a reasonable bonus—call it hazardous duty pay, or whatever—we could agree on a quit-claim to donate our compensation from the Russians to any fund they designate. As is, where is, and as we received it. I mainly want to embarrass that chicken-shit colonel that gave me a hard time."

Neeta chimed in. "And if they find that it's not genuine, we could suggest they press charges against the Russians. We had no way to verify the bills out in the boonies."

"Actually," I said, "I pulled a couple of the bills yesterday and looked them over. They looked right to me—really first-class work. Shelikov might be teasing us, and the money genuine."

"I don't wanna hear that," said Mike. "I'd wander around for the next ten years waiting for a hand on my shoulder. I'd rather assume he did put one over on us, and just get rid of the bills."

I tended to agree. If the bills were good, the Army came out ahead. If they were queer, let the colonel figure out what to do. I suspected he'd find a way to sweep it all under the carpet.

Liz came home about martini time; I made her one from the leavings of our test bottle, but I let her drink alone. I and the partners had taken full advantage of Shelikov's generosity and I didn't need any more. Mike and Neeta had long since hauled their crates of vodka to Eagle River in Mike's truck.

"Any new pieces to your serial killer puzzle?" I asked, when she had settled down to her after-work relaxer.

"The locals were too slow picking up on the possibility that one person was doing most of the damage," she complained. "Earlier attempts at abductions were seen as one-offs, and were investigated as such. Now, looking back, it almost appears as though several assaults and kidnapping attempts were clumsy practice moves."

"Anything at all on the early attempts that might tie to the guy that's doing the current killings?"

"Only by stretching the imagination," she replied. "See what you can make of this."

"Over five years ago, a guy in a truck grabs a young woman off the street. He drives her down on the Kenai, beats her a little bit and pulls off the rape. He gets the names of her parents, tells her that he'll kill them if she reports the incident. She reports it anyway, gives the cops the description and license number of the truck. Cops talk to the man; he claims she consented and wasn't happy with the fee, threatened to call the police and claim rape.

"Police have a he-said, she-said situation and no proof of anything. They let the guy go.

"A month later, a woman complains that a man tried to pick her up off the street, but she managed to escape. Same guy, and he claims a misunderstanding—he was just trying to ask her for a date and she took it wrong. Again, he-said, she-said, no evidence.

"Several cops put this guy on their 'ass-hole' list, figuring that if it happens again, they'll squeeze until something pops."

"There's another similar incident. No positive ID this time, but a strong probability it's the same guy. They look closer at this guy, find that he runs a small business, is liked, and trusted by those who know him, and is in no way the killer-rapist type. Wife and kids, active in church and community."

"Any record of arrests other than those?"

"A few shoplifting busts, most of which he talked his way out of. This is a soft-spoken man with a plausible explanation for everything."

She paused, took a few sips of her martini, and continued.

"Over the next year, the bodies of three women were found near Anchorage. One dumped near the Eklutna Lake road, one near the old Knik River bridge, and one off the Seward Highway near Girdwood. Two were obviously dumped after death; the third had her hands bound and may have died trying to escape."

"Any evidence connecting them with your first suspect?" I asked.

"None whatsoever. Looks like a new player in town. About a year after that, hunters found a woman's body partly buried on the Knik River flats. That stirred up some interest and a few more were discovered, all shot and buried in places where a plane could have landed but where ground access was difficult."

"Any new suspects?"

"In a city where everyone has a pickup truck and a rifle, and hundreds own light aircraft or hold pilots' licenses, the cops had all the suspects they needed—just no clues or evidence pointing to any of them! I couldn't even try my personality profiling without someone to compare it against."

"You look tired," I said. "Let me cook up something while you relax. We can hit the sack early tonight. Maybe your intuition will kick in during the night and you'll have a new angle in the morning."

CHAPTER 54

Compromise

Liz was lost in thought through most of breakfast. I could see why these cases were getting to her—most FBI cases involved bank robberies, high level financial scams, espionage, and other crimes that allowed objective scrutiny from an impersonal distance. Liz was now looking closely at deliberate torture, rape, and murder for the sole purpose of satisfying an evil craving.

She had brought home files showing mutilated corpses, half exhumed bodies, women naked or largely so, with hand trussed behind their backs and bullet-shattered skulls. She was seeing the aftermath of purposeful violence, and seeing it face to face. She was seeing autopsy photos in which science was pitted against savagery in an attempt to obtain justice for the poor pitiful thing lying on a cold morgue slab.

I could see a pressure building under Liz's usually calm demeanor, a tenseness which was eroding her customary kindness and good humor. She was building a hate for any sub-animal creatures which were capable of such crimes.

"No flashes of insight during the night?" I asked after pouring her second cup of coffee. She shook her head.

"Ben, I can't figure the 'why' of it all. Any man in this town who wants sex has only to walk down 4th Avenue with 50 bucks in his wallet. Why would such a guy go to all the trouble, expense, and risk to do these things to women?"

"I don't know," I said. "I'd bet that if there were no women available, he'd find something else to torture."

"But I had one thought," I continued. "This guy or these guys pick street-walkers, show girls and bar girls—basically women considered low class trash in average circles. I'll bet these killers are church-raised or otherwise of a class that would look down on such women. Therefore, they can look on them without the empathy they might have for a daughter, wife, or girlfriend. They can treat the victims as though they deserve anything that happens to them, just because of their lifestyle."

"That ties in with a lot of the things I learned in the FBI human behavioral courses. Maybe you should become a profiler?"

"I think I'd rather be an exterminator," I said, "and rid the world of assholes like that after you identify 'em."

"I'm leaning that way myself after looking over some of these case files. But now I'd better go to work. There's a crusty old Trooper Sergeant I need to talk to. They tell me he's an oddball character, but he's cleared some tough cases by thinking out of the box. Maybe his intuition is better than mine."

I watched her nondescript government sedan disappear up my lane and silently wished her luck.

Jim McGann showed up a little before noon, probably assuming he'd get a free lunch out of the deal. Without actually saying so, I implied that I had just eaten, willing to suffer a little hunger to enjoy Jim's.

"Here're the four ledgers you found for us," he said. "The Russians didn't try any elaborate cypher system—just a few simple books that our observers probably wouldn't have noticed were it not for handcuffing the briefcase to the Colonel's wrist."

"From what you told me, and what I picked up from Major Jordan's Diaries, I'd guess the Soviets were making a last-minute effort at getting out while the getting was good."

"Good guess. They'd been smuggling sleeper agents, moles if you want to call them that, into the country for years using the Lend-Lease pipeline. These ledgers contained a master list of their agents' names, aliases, and destinations in the US. You'll notice that any one book revealed nothing—a list of Russian names, a list of localities in the States, a list of numbers, or a list of American or English names."

"Don't wanna steal your punch line," I said, "but seemed to me that one or two books are useless. But if you look at any single line, and its corresponding line in all the other books—if you had the other books—you just might come up with the agent's control number, his or her Russian name, his or her adopted American name, and the community in which they were embedded."

"Well," said McGann, "if you figured it out that easily, it wasn't much of a code. Anyhow, even after 30 years, it's valuable to us. Quite a few names are still in place and are viable sleeper agents. A few have decided that fading into the community as US citizens was preferable to returning to the USSR as temporary heroes. A few have been caught due to carelessness."

"I can see why you didn't want the Soviets to know we had the info," I said. "They would have just closed shop and pulled out their people. Now, you guys can keep tabs on them, filter what intelligence you want them to have, and uncover the chains of contacts that keep them functional. Now you have a window into their bedrooms."

"I wouldn't put it just that way, Ben, but after the Fuchs and Greenglass surprises a few years back, it's nice to have some kind of feel for where the copperheads are lying in the weeds."

"OK," I said. "Now we know we done good; we fulfilled our contract. What do your bosses say about the 200 grand that they'd like to get their hands on?"

"They want it, naturally. The Judge Advocate General is of the opinion that you have no entitlement to the payment because you had no legal entitlement to the airplane. There's some logic there, after all."

"Maybe, but the international laws of salvage are pretty complex. He might be in over his head. It would take a long fight in the courts to settle it. And probably some publicity. In fact, I can damn well guarantee the publicity."

"The boss colonel, the one you like to call number two for some reason that I won't explore, tends to agree. He concedes that since you actually did get into a fire-fight, maybe two if I read your confusing report right, and your crew were held at gunpoint by hostile forces, you should all be given a commendation for valor and service to your country."

About the time I puffed up and was about to rain all over his commendation, he added, "And a special bonus for hazardous duty above and beyond, etc."

My next question was short. "How much?"

His reply was nearly as short. "Double your daily fee and an extra thousand for you for getting shot."

I immediately felt a warm spot in my heart for number two.

"Tell him I believe him most generous. We agree, and I will write up the terms of our quit-claim now."

CHAPTER 55

The Little Weasel

Liz came dragging in in worse shape, figuratively speaking, than the previous day.

"Dammit," she exclaimed as she came through the door. "They found another body today. Fresh. Some passing pilot noticed tracks from a fat-tired Super Cub on a gravel bar about half way to Knik glacier. Called in a Trooper helicopter and found a new grave and a body not 48 hours old."

"New details?"

"Not very new. Shot with a 223 and he threw the empty into the grave with her. Looked like sperm on her outer clothing. They do expect to get an ID though. Everything fresh and teeth intact.

"How about your first suspect—the guy that gets away on he-said, she-said situations?"

"They'll be checking him for alibies tomorrow, but he'll be clean."

"You're sure?"

"He always is. Pals around with a couple of local sportsmen. They hunt together, fish together, fly together—I think they must even go to the john together."

"Fly together?"

"Yeah, they have airplanes. They'll take a pair of small planes and spend a weekend hunting wolves or fishing isolated streams across the inlet. Must be nice to be able to afford that kind of recreation."

"Well, if he eliminates himself as a suspect, at least it narrows the field—you'll know to look somewhere else."

She gave me a weary look. "If there was a somewhere else. Ben, we have absolutely nothing that points to anybody. And the only thing that points to the first suspect is that old pair of he-said she-said incidents."

"Does he have an airplane?"

"Owns a Super Cub but doesn't have a pilot's license; couldn't pass the flight physical for some reason. I pretty sure he's clean on this, Ben. He must have learned his lesson with those encounters years ago."

"Did you get any ideas from the oddball Trooper Sergeant you mentioned?"

"Oh, he hates the 'he-said, she-said' guy; he's been convinced from the start that, 'The little weasel did it, and he's still doing it!'. I think I read in the files where that Sergeant did the initial interview after the first incident. Said, 'The smell of death is on him.', or something to that effect."

"Hard to charge a man who has a cast-iron alibi," I observed. "Find somebody else or you'll go crazy. Any means of checking out the Super Cubs that flew out of Merrill Field during the hours in question?"

"Probably a hundred," she answered, "and half didn't file a flight plan. Alaskans don't seem to pay much attention to regulatory requirements, even when they're for their own safety."

"Well, you can eliminate the half that did—nobody's gonna file a flight plan when they're heading out to dispose of a body."

She brightened. "Good point, Sherlock. I'll see if there is a log of takeoffs and landings by tail number. Subtract those with a flight plan and subtract those who're just practicing touch-and-goes and we might come up with a manageable list."

"And," I added, "you might look closer at those that left after dark or at times when there were few people to notice what was being loaded into their Cub."

Somewhat mellowed after discovering a new direction for her investigation, Liz accepted a slightly hot-rodded vodka martini and we settled back on the sofa for an hour's relaxation before supper (Dinner for her; we had argued over the distinction between supper and dinner for years. Now, we ate the same meal, I calling it supper and she, dinner. Both seemed to taste about the same to me.)

Liz spent most of her next day with her counterparts in the APD and the Troopers. I spent mine at the Isaac Walton shooting range near Birchwood. After the rough treatment my Winchester and the Smith & Wesson pocket pistol had received in the north country, I wanted to check function and zero of both.

The 338 Winchester needed a few clicks of windage and elevation to get the zero on at 200 yards. Function seemed unimpaired—the rifle fed from the magazine perfectly from any position, including upside down.

The pistol had fixed sights, so zero wasn't a problem. I did want to check that the heavy high-speed loads that had so nicely ripped into Gushkov's gas tank hadn't shaken anything loose.

Mike Gearhart showed up, as planned, with his brand new 300 Weatherby and a box of ammunition.

"I'm surprised you could find a new Weatherby in Anchorage," I said. "They're pretty fancy guns for beating around in this country."

"Mountain View Sporting Goods had a couple," he said. "There's a little demand from wealthy eastern hunters who think shinier means better. I just like their flat trajectory and longer usable range."

"Hell, Mike, the further away you shoot 'em, the longer the walk to clean'em and pack 'em out". There was no real logic to my statement, but it gave me the chance to get in the last word.

Mike just ignored me and set about zeroing the new rifle for 300 yards. When he was finished, I followed him back to his Eagle River home and updated him and Neeta on the deal I had made with the CIC.

They were happy with the doubling of the daily fee, and when I explained how I had worded the quit-claims I had brought along for their signatures, they seemed less anxious about the long arm of the government unexpectedly reaching out. Jim was to drop over after work and pick them up, delivering in exchange fresh checks reflecting our new pay scale.

I drove home happy, and hoping that Liz had accomplished something that would bring her home in a better mood.

CHAPTER 56

A Cozy Evening

"Well," I asked when Liz came in the front door, "was your Wednesday any better than your Tuesday?"
"Make me a drink."
"I guess that means no," I said.
"It does."
"Name your poison."
"The good scotch."
"Shame to waste that on a pissed-off FBI agent," I said. "Why don't we go out and have a steak, some decent wine, and finish up with a tot of Drambuie?"
"OK, we'll do that—but I want a scotch now."
I gave in, which was usually the case, and poured her three fingers of single malt, adding an ice cube. Suspecting that she might overdo the drinking if she remained in her present mood, I made myself a light one and settled down to listen.
"Ben, it's so damn frustrating! I just spent a year getting all these new skills pumped into me, and I can't use 'em. We just haven't been able to come up with a suspect to concentrate on. If we had one, we could glue a tail on him until we were proved right or wrong. If we came up with several, I could apply profiling and maybe narrow it down."
"Let's go back to the beginning and start over," I said. "Your oddball Trooper settled on the first suspect and won't let go. Why? He has no evidence."
"Says he doesn't believe in coincidence. The same guy twice,

maybe, but the probable third time, uh uh. And his gut tells him that the guy is slimy bad."

"And you can't see it.?"

"No, maybe the guy's just a slow learner."

'Or maybe a fast learner', I thought to myself.

"Liz, let's get a time line on the she-said, he-said incidents, including the unproven probable. Then the approximate death dates of the women who were found dumped around Anchorage. Finally, the best guesses on the death dates of the ones who were found buried out on the gravel bars."

Her interest perked up by my questions, she put down her scotch and went to the files she had brought home for study. A few minutes later, I heard an exclamation and Liz plopped down beside me on the sofa.

"Look at this, Ben. The first suspect made three tries that we know about, all unsuccessful, and was positively identified during two of them. Shortly afterward, we start finding the roadside bodies. Not much of a chance of IDing the perp on those murders because the witnesses were dead. The only clues were a few people who saw a generic pickup cruising the area of the abduction or of the body dump. Nothing positive."

"What else," I asked.

"No more bodies found along the roads. But the estimated kill dates on the gravel bar murders show them as almost a continuation of the road side kill sequence."

"So maybe the same killer updating his methods?" I asked.

"I think so," she said excitedly. "And look at this—the original suspect bought and registered his Super Cub between the roadside kill dates and the gravel bar kill dates."

"Of course, none of this is evidence," I said, "and you told me he doesn't have a pilot's license, but does have an iron-clad alibi."

"In the morning," she said, "I'm gonna check with the Merrill Field tower and follow up on the Cub take off activity we talked about yesterday. I have a hunch we might open up something of value.

"So, forget the steak, Ben. I'm feeling pretty good right now. Another drink, if I ever finish this one, and I'll whip up something for us here. Fall chill is starting earlier in the evenings now; why don't you build us a fire for us to hang around after dinner. I'll get out of this darn suit and into something comfortable."

The tide had certainly turned in the last 15 minutes, and definitely for the better. I looked forward to a cozy evening.

When Jim McGann rapped on the door the next morning, Liz was long gone and I was just finishing a late breakfast. I offered him coffee, which he seemed anxious to accept.

"Ben, if I keep on dealing with you, I'll need more than coffee to get jump started in the mornings." He dropped his briefcase on the floor, swung a leg over the kitchen chair, and squared himself with the cup I had set before him.

"Colonel number two—and I'm starting to realize why you call him that—got chinchy all of a sudden. Asked me if I thought we could trim the bonus checks some more without you and your friends raising a stink."

"And you said?"

"I said, 'Dammit, Colonel, that guy Hunnicutt got shot trying to complete this job. Getting shot at wasn't a part of his contract, and getting hit damn sure wasn't.' I said that you'd likely raise a stink, and if you pursued the matter there'd have to be an investigation that would probably leak to the public."

He scooped up his briefcase and laid it on the table, open.

"Gimme the money and the quit-claims. I need to get this over and start a very early long weekend before he thinks of something else."

I retrieved the original Russian satchel containing the cash, the quit-claims for the C-47, and the signed quit-claims for the cash. The rope Gushkov had used for a shoulder strap was still attached, and a few shreds of jerky were stuck to the interior. The spatters of blood on the exterior were my own; I had left them untouched as evidence that I had nearly given my all for my country.

Jim handed over the bonus checks, for which I thanked him very nicely and bade him farewell at the front door.

I hoped he wouldn't get into any trouble if the money was actually counterfeit, but I had a lot of faith in Colonel number two's ability sweep anything embarrassing under the bureaucratic carpet.

CHAPTER 57

Timetable for Murder

I piddled around the house for a while before checking that Mike Gearhart and Neeta were home. The news of the bonus checks brought an immediate invitation for lunch, instantly accepted, naturally. Neeta kept a pretty good moose stew ready for action.

I drove out the Glenn Highway to the Eagle River turn off and up the twisting road to Mike's cabin, high on the north wall of the valley. Before knocking, I turned and absorbed the astounding view of the river, the town tenuously attached to the highway, and the great Alaska Range banked up behind Mount Susitna to the west.

I knew the bluff behind my own home furnished the finest view for a hundred miles, but I had to concede second place to Mike's front porch. When the valley became crowded enough to push Mike out, he should be able to sell his building lot for a small fortune.

Many of the old timers were finding themselves crowded beyond their comfort level, and were trading the old homesteads for very comfortable retirement elsewhere. I recalled the saying by one old prospector I had known; "The first person in the valley is called a pioneer—the next is a damn squatter!"

The "bonus" checks, which honesty would have called extortion checks, were well received. Even the best paid pipeline workers weren't apt to clear 14 thousand for a week's work—of course, they weren't expected to face armed Russians, either.

The stew lived up to expectations, the coffee was good (Mike actually provided sugar and cream now, due to the softening influence of tiny Neeta), and the conversation was pleasant and relaxed. For the first time since the expedition was formed, we had nothing ominous or worrying hanging over us; the most serious concerns being how the pay would be spent.

That question was of little importance to me. There was nothing I needed and my truck was good for another year or two. Mike and Neeta, however, were newlyweds in a sense, although the word wedding hadn't been mentioned. There was talk of adding a guest room, maybe a car port or garage so Neeta didn't have to scrape winter ice from her truck, and a small utility space for a washer and dryer.

The conversation eventually becoming uncomfortably domestic, I decided to take my leave. I knew that I would soon be asked about Liz, how long would she stay, and what would we do when she had to leave. In my mind, I had avoided those very same questions every hour of every day, and had no intention of being forced to consider the possibly painful answers until the very last second.

Liz arrived home in a more hopeful frame of mind than I had seen in a while.

"I spun out the timeline of the probable kill dates and showed how they might lead to an evolving pattern of murder by a single person," she said. "My partners saw some sense in it and we're gonna dig deeper. The Trooper Sergeant especially liked it. He still swears the little weasel he first interviewed is the bad guy."

"You still have to break what you called a cast iron alibi," I said. "Or consider that he didn't do the ones he had an alibi for. Did your timeline for the kill dates point to any precise interval, or any particular days of the week?"

"The older bodies couldn't be pinpointed as to time of death. Best guesses gave a week-long time bracket. The medical examiner's a guy named Don Rogers, and he's sharp as a tack. Doc Rogers looks at a lot of stuff I wouldn't have thought of—the life cycle and span of bugs and larvae found on the body, rate of deterioration of clothing materials in the grave environment, even the amount of tarnishing on the brass cartridge cases found in the graves.

"But the cops say that if he gives a 5-day bracket on time of death, it'll likely turn out to be near the center of that bracket.

"The fresh ones, of course, he can call right down to the day."

"OK," I said, "centering the kill dates along the time line as best you can, any pattern?"

She opened her briefcase and shook out some folders and a long sheet of graph paper. She took my martini off the kitchen table, stole a long swallow from it, and replaced it with the spread-out graph paper.

We both scrutinized it at some length. She marked the positive dates with a red dot, the bracketed dates with a red dot in the center of the bracket.

"Now let's fill in the days of the week," I suggested.

Labelling the long graph with the days of the week took a little time, but before she was finished, we could see a trend forming.

"The positive kill days either hit or cluster around Saturdays and Sundays," Liz said. "The killer either works a five-day week, or he likes to hit the strips when there are big, drunk Saturday night crowds and people are less apt to remember anything unusual happening."

"How about the interval between known kills," I asked. She pointed wordlessly. The positive kill days were either six weekends or twelve weekends apart.

"The skipped weekends might mean he skipped a kill for some reason," she said, "or that we just haven't found a body yet."

"I don't know," I said. "If his compulsion to kill peaked every six weeks and he had to miss one, I think he'd try harder the next weekend. I think the skipped sixth weekends represent bodies you haven't yet found."

CHAPTER 58

Merrill Field

Liz left for work the next morning anxious to show our timeline work to her fellow wizards. If the killer did succumb to his impulses every six weekends, and the first known killings had taken place four years ago, there were a lot more bodies out there.

I had neglected to turn in the special blue Federal ID that McGann had issued me, so decided to poke around Merrill Field this morning to see what further data might be available to us. A friendly conversation with one of the tower controllers during his break yielded the information that tower procedures were a bit informal in The Last Frontier. Many pilots using the field were from villages with bush strips; they might not come to the big city for months at a time and never became familiar with regulatory matters. A flight plan might be a short radio message, "Hey, tower. This is Barney Ruggles headed back to Kaltag."

Even local flyers tended to be careless about aircraft type and tail numbers when requesting takeoff and landing instructions. Much of this was probably due to the fact that the small community of flyers from previous decades knew one another, recognized the various airplanes, and didn't see any need to get formal about it. The location of the old tower precluded the controllers from getting any kind of view of most small planes as they taxied to the runway.

In any case, I was informed that it would be impossible to get individual takeoff and landing data that would stand up in court—especially if the defense counsel was a pilot and knew the ropes, which most were.

When Liz came home that afternoon, she was a little discouraged at how slowly the wheels of justice rotated in our city. Terms like "probable cause" and "due process" which she had used so lightly in the past were dragging down the process of the investigation. The fact that their only suspect operated a successful neighborhood grocery business and was married with children scared the hell out of potential prosecutors. If he was found innocent after being publicly charged, careers could be fatally damaged, both in the APD and the attorney general's office.

"Liz, get me the tail number of this guy's Super Cub and find out where it's tied down. I want to look it over."

"Ben, I can't search the plane without a warrant, and I can't get a warrant without probable cause."

"Then don't search the damn plane. Just find out where it is. And look at your timeline and tell me where on the calendar the next six-week interval falls."

"You're going to stake it out on that weekend?" she asked.

"Yeah, and you should get the cops to tail what's-his-name if he goes out to make the rounds.

"By the way, what the hell is his name? I know you guys have been holding it close for a number of good reasons, but I'd sure like to know who I'm stalking."

She pondered for a minute, obviously reluctant, but finally turned to me and spoke in a low voice.

"His name's Whimple; Charley Whimple. Runs an upscale grocery store in a little strip mall on Muldoon. He's so respectable, it hurts. Drives a tan '69 Plymouth four-door sedan or a green Jeep pickup. But if you get caught poking around in his business and screw up this case for us, Buster, you'd better find a stable to sleep in."

Liz phoned me the aircraft information I had requested around mid-morning. I made it a point to lunch at Peggy's restaurant, just across the street from Merrill Field. Early in the afternoon I went over to the field and strolled around examining the various parked planes. The walk was interesting in itself—

the planes varied from surplus military aircraft and warbirds to homebuilt contraptions with names like "Deathtrap II" and "Kitchen sink".

Most prevalent were light short-strip machines like the Super Cub and smaller Cessnas, but a number of twin-engine jobs were present. Useful, I imagined for freight and passenger hauling between the larger airports.

I found the designated tie-down for Whimple's Cub; the plane was there, relatively clean, and apparently ready for flight. I would have expected an unused plane to show dirt, dust, and foggy windows, with built-up surface residue from the constant winds. Whether he had a license or not, Whimple or someone else had been flying this plane.

I peered inside, searching for anything unusual or different, but it appeared to be a typical Alaskan fat-tired bush plane. If it had been landed often on the Knik gravel bars, the fat doughnut tires would certainly have been needed.

As I started to walk away, I was struck by an odd difference in the latching system of the cabin doors. Looking more closely, I could see that the inside latching handles had been modified so that they could only be operated from the front, or pilot's position. A Cub is not the easiest airplane to get in or out of; the flimsy and odd-shaped half-door arrangement requires some dexterity and flexibility to climb through. Every door modification I had seen was designed to make entry and exit easier and faster, certainly not to impede it.

With this particular modification, any crash that killed or knocked out the pilot would leave the rear seat passenger trapped, at least until he or she found a way to rip the doors loose from the airframe. That made no sense. It seemed clear to me that the modification was meant to block any exit—or escape—from the rear seat until the pilot was ready.

Although this was a condemning piece of evidence in my mind, I knew it was only personal conjecture and would never hold up in court. From what I had heard of Whimple, his soft voice could conjure up a "dog ate my homework" explanation that could convince almost any skeptic.

Another odd thing that I only noted as I began to walk away— Whimple's tie-down spot was near the end of the parking area. It was easy to drive to, but away from the security lights which gave at least partial illumination to most of the other tie-downs. Since there were plenty of vacant spaces in the lighted areas, why had Whimple chosen one in a darkened area?

CHAPTER 59

Stake-Out

Before leaving the field, I located several Cessna side-by-side airplanes tied down in positions to observe Wimple's Cub from a discrete distance. Revisiting my friend from the control tower, I asked the names and contact info of their owners.

"Interested in buying a private plane?" he asked, while looking up the information. I almost laughed at the thought of owning a plane, considering my distaste for flying.

"Nope. I have a friend who might be—just thought I'd give him something to think about."

That evening, I told Liz of my day's work and invited her comments.

"Are you thinking of staking out Wimple's Cub on one of the time-line kill dates?" she asked.

"The next one, if we're figuring correctly on his build-up periods, would be next weekend. If we're off by a week, it'll be tomorrow. If we wait, it'll be over a month until he's ready again and somebody may die between times. Seems to me that catching him in the act would be a lot more definitive than months of piling up a stack of circumstantial evidence that the court might throw out."

"You're right on the in-the-act bit," she said. "We can't know where he'll pick up his next victim, or where he might fly her, but if we can catch him forcing her into his truck or plane, we should have him. His alibies for previous killings won't matter."

"Here is a list of plane owners who have tie-downs in good

spots for staking out Whimple's Cub. See if you can get your cops to contact them and get permission for us to use their planes to sit and wait." I handed her the list I received from the controller.

"If you can get the OK for that, I'll drive you over early in the morning and show you the layout. Then I'll sit stakeout tomorrow afternoon and through the night. If nothing happens, I'll do it again next week."

She was in quiet thought for a few minutes, then went to the phone and spent 15 minutes talking to her police partners. While she was on the phone, I made us drinks and started a meat loaf cooking.

When she picked up her martini, she said she'd have to wait for a call-back, but that there should be no problem with stakeout people using the airplanes in question.

The call came quickly enough, and she was apparently satisfied with the results.

"Three of the four airplane owners gave permission for us to use their planes." She showed me the list with one name lined out.

"A scruffy undercover narc they call 'Eddie B.' will tail the guy if he leaves home. Ed will have a radio, and so will I. He'll call me with update info as he follows Wimple, so if he tries to bring a woman to his plane, we'll know he's on the way. We'll have no way to know if the trip is voluntary on her part except by observing their behavior."

"We'd better be damn sure before we act," I said. "If we screw it up, we've killed the whole investigation."

At five fifteen on Saturday, Liz was hunkered down in the front seat of a Cessna parked a row down and one over from our suspect's Cub. She had a clear view from a distance of not more than 40 feet. I was the same distance away on the opposite side from Liz.

At exactly six PM, Liz got a call that Whimple had left home and was headed toward the Spenard district. Although located across town from the 4th Avenue watering holes, Spenard had a thriving red-light village that had been in operation long before the pipeline was even imagined.

According to Eddie, Whimple entered several Spenard nightspots over the next hour and always left alone. Eventually, he left another, but hung around the parking lot for 15 minutes, obviously waiting for someone. The woman who finally came out by a side door was in her twenties and didn't appear as shopworn as might be expected. She climbed into the passenger seat of his Jeep truck, leaned over and kissed him, and settled back for the ride.

Eddie stuck onto their tail until it was plain that they were headed toward Merrill, then looped around and approached by a different route to give us backup. I watched as a pair of headlights approached from the direction of Airport Heights and slowly made its way toward our section of the tie-down rows.

It was a green pickup; it eased closer and parked near the tail of Whimple's Super Cub. Both Liz and I had opened the doors or windows of the plane we occupied to insure we could hear as much conversation as possible.

"Hey," came the woman's voice, "you offered three hundred bucks to pose for nude pictures—you didn't say anything about flying anywhere."

"I thought I told you," came a soft male voice. "I've got a cabin on a lake about 20 minutes out of town. I like taking the nude shots in a natural setting, maybe some on a porch swing and others lounging on a rustic rail with the lake in the background. And maybe some others," he said in a suggestive tone, "when we're into the stash I've hidden out there."

I heard a door open and a man stepped out of the truck and walked around to the passenger side.

"Look," he said, in a wheedling voice, "you've got a helluva body. I'm willing to pay four hundred, but it's gotta be at the cabin. That's where my cameras and lighting equipment are stored."

The woman hesitated, then evidently made a decision.

"No, I'm not gonna go flying around the bush just for 400 bucks. I can make that easy back at the club. I was just hoping for a relaxed night with no north slopers pawing at me. Take me back to the..."

There was a thud and a scuffle, and I could see the struggling woman being dragged over to the plane. I started to move in that direction, but remembered that we had to make very sure that the lady's departure was not voluntary.

CHAPTER 60

Shoot Out

Whimple was clumsily wrapping her arms and face with duct tape as he dragged her, and only a few panicky sounds escaped. He opened the right-side doors of the Cub and literally stuffed her writhing body into the cramped rear seat. Reaching into his jacket, he produced a large revolver and pressed it against her temple.

"What I'm going to do to you can be done just as well with you dead," he said. "Now behave and I'll let you go when I'm finished with you. It's just picture taking. But give me any trouble at all and I'll shoot you and dump your body out at 5000 feet."

She quieted and he walked back to the truck, pulled a canvas bag from behind the seat, and returned to the Cub. Stuffing the revolver back under his jacket, he extracted a large odd appearing pistol from the bag. It was a special TC single-shot pistol equipped with a telescopic sight and a long barrel, and designed for long-range pistol hunting. I was willing to bet that it was in 223 caliber.

I slipped out of my hiding spot as quietly as I could and drew my GI 45 automatic from the tanker holster across my chest. I was about to call on Whimple to drop the gun and get on the ground when I heard Liz's icy voice demand the same. He hesitated.

"Do it now or I will kill you where you stand." I had never heard her speak in that voice before—cold, flat, and with an inflection of hate.

He gently put the big TC down, careful not to scratch it on the hardstand, and stood looking at her.

"You've got it all wrong, ma'am. The lady is a bit doped up and I had to secure her so she didn't interfere while I was flying her home." His soft, sincere words were almost convincing. I knew that he'd go for the revolver the second he realized he was not believed. I silently eased the safety off the 45 and lined my sights up on his belt buckle, ready to stop the fight before it started.

"Look," he said, "I'm an EMT. I'll show you my credentials." He reached toward his jacket pocket.

My mind told my trigger finger to act, but before the impulse was obeyed, Liz's Magnum hammered out four shots with scarcely an interval between. Whimple buckled forward, caught himself, and stood swaying, looking at Liz with an incredulous expression on his face.

Two more slugs caught him in the throat; with a final gurgle, he fell backward, face-up on the tarmac. At that instant, light flooded the scene as Ed, our back-up, came to a skidding stop, headlamps blazing.

I made it to the body ahead of Ed and pushed back its jacket. I closed Whimple's dead hand over the butt of his revolver and pulled the undrawn gun free of its place in his waistband, leaving it in Whimple's outstretched hand.

"He's dead," I announced, perhaps unnecessarily, and turned my attention to the girl imprisoned in the Super Cub. I first peeled the duct tape from across her mouth, reassuring her all the while that she would be OK, that no one could harm her now; that her ordeal was over.

As soon as I had freed her arms, she clutched at me, whimpering unintelligibly—when others approached, she flinched away and buried herself deeper in my arms. I held her and soothed her as best I could. I couldn't begin to imagine her emotions after the events of the last few minutes.

The ruckus on Merrill Field had set all the first responders in motion. The police were all over us, as well as the ambulance and fire truck from a station that was only a few blocks away. I noted a big State Trooper Sergeant standing in the background, scrutinizing the scene, taking notes, and looking very satisfied.

When the medics tried to take the victim in for treatment and observation, she panicked and fought them off, clinging to me.

Liz approached and asked the medics if I might accompany the victim to the ER, as I seemed the only person at the scene that she trusted. When they assented, Liz pushed both me and the victim into the ambulance and waved it away.

    This was the first opportunity I had to see the woman in good light. Small in stature, maybe five feet four, with a finely sculptured face and chestnut hair, she couldn't have been more than 25 years old. Even in her battered condition, she was pretty—I think a few years of maturity would have added real beauty. Her figure would be considered ideal by those of us who prefer rounded contours. If Whimple had taken his pictures, they would have been hum-dingers.

    At the ER, she was found to have bruises and a few cuts and scrapes from being crammed into the Super Cub, but appeared physically sound. We still faced panic every time I started to leave, so the ER nurse asked if I would stay with her until their sedatives took hold. I told the nurse about the victim's terrible ordeal, and asked if they would be sure to have some sympathetic soul present when she woke.

    I had been beside the girl during most of the ER's preliminary examination, she clinging to my hand and looking fearfully at the strange people that surrounded her. When she finally drifted off, I went out to the parking lot to find Liz and a cop waiting for me. We sat in a police car while the cop took my statement as to the events of the evening. Liz then drove me home and we both over-imbibed while reliving the day's events.

    The next morning required a visit to the police station and a more thorough interrogation by a new pair of cops. Their questioning might have been embarrassing had I not anticipated it and mentally rehearsed some answers between drinks last night.

    As to why I had been at the scene, I showed the mysterious blue ID to them and said it was a federal matter. They later checked with Liz who merely nodded and walked away. The question of being armed during the encounter was soon dismissed, as I had shown that the 1911 Colt was carried openly in an exposed holster, in strict accordance with Alaska law. The small snub-nosed 38 that had been hidden in my boot top was definitely concealed and against the law, but since it was never mentioned, I saw no need of bringing it up.

Asking for the shooting scene pictures, I pointed out the modified door latches as a sure indication that the encounter was definitely intended to be a kidnapping.

When asked if I would have fired at the deceased, I admitted that I was prepared to do so, but that my interference had not been required.

They finally came to the crux of the matter.

"Did Agent Nichole fire in self-defense?"

"Yes. She instructed the suspect to disarm and lie down on the blacktop. He did not do so. When his hand moved under his jacket, she fired."

"Would you have fired under those conditions?"

"Yes. I started to, but her reflexes were quicker."

"Did you actually see a gun?"

"When I checked to see if the suspect was dead, a large revolver was in his hand."

"Thank you, Sir. That will be all."

CHAPTER 61

Aftermath

The next week was hard on both Liz and on me. Hard on her because she filled days doing reports and paperwork, and on gathering data to be used to refine the new profiling system that she was helping develop. On me because, with the Red Star business taken care of, and Liz on her own, I was bored to death.

There were actually a few distracting incidents—the good ole' boys that had given Whimple his iron-clad alibi were forced to recant, and the resultant publicity made them extremely unpopular with the public. But, according to the liars, good ole' Charley had told them he needed cover because he was stepping out on his wife. Why that made it OK, I wasn't sure, but it did seem to mollify the hunting crowd to a degree; the fact that their preventing him from being caught earlier probably cost the lives of half-dozen women didn't seem to bother them. My faith in the basic goodness of humanity was taking a beating lately.

A map of south-central Alaska was found in Charley's home. Experts scoured it for some indication where he might have killed and buried his victims, but found no marks. Then one of the crew held it to the light and noticed dozens of tiny pin-prick holes. The location of some holes very precisely matched locations where bodies had already been found.

These tiny holes were transferred to other maps and search parties began finding Charley's victims, one by one.

A week after the shooting, Liz took me out for seafood, treated me to my favorite Moselle wine, then cornered me on the sofa soon after we arrived home.

"Ben, I've got to talk to somebody about that shooting, and I guess you drew the short straw."

"I know, Liz, and you don't really have to say anything."

"What do you mean, you know? You don't have the slightest idea!"

"All right, Liz. Let's not talk around it. You feel unprofessional; you think you killed Whimple because you wanted to—not because he was going for his gun. You're wondering if that makes you the same kind of person that he was."

She stared at me accusingly, dropped her eyes to her lap, and began to weep quietly.

"If you know it, then everyone else probably does. And if I really did, I need to get out of this line of work."

I took her in my arms and let her tears wet down my collar for a minute or two. Then I looked into her eyes.

"Liz, you were too quick for me. I was looking for his hand to go for his revolver, and my sights were on his belt buckle. I fully intended to kill him the second he moved, or maybe a second later if he didn't move. I wasn't about to let that guy live, no matter what."

"But I don't know if I really saw him move," she said, "or if I imagined it so I would have an excuse to shoot. But when I realized that I had put four in him, and he was dead on his feet, why did I shoot him again?"

"To be sure he was dead," I said. "The same reason I would have put a 45 in him if he had so much as twitched. Listen to my story for a while, Liz, then we can come back to yours."

I told her about Nikolay Gushkov, all about Nikolay Gushkov, from his rude introduction to Neeta, his insistence on taking her when he fled, his casual killing of Sherry Jensen because he didn't want to argue about taking her truck, his shooting and pistol-whipping of the pair at the Glennallen gas station.

"I wanted him dead, Liz, and I didn't especially want to be merciful about it. When Stripe and I set up the roadblock, I never thought about doing it any other way. I loaded the pistol with a couple of stoppers, and without even debating to myself about it, I backed 'em up with a couple of flare shells. I didn't know he'd charge us—figured he'd fort-up in the truck or run for the bush.

"When I aimed at him, I don't think I missed—I think I probably aimed for the gas tank. When I fired the flares, I think I got the results I hoped for. I say 'I think', because I really don't recall planning his incineration; I did what I did, step after step, without thought or planning. I felt neither relief nor sorrow when I watched him burn."

I paused. She looked at me, her face showing both pity and pain.

"So, it happened to you too. You took justice, bent it to your own ends, and arbitrarily administered it in your own fashion. Just as I did with Whimple. What are we turning into Ben?"

"I think we're just being human. Each of us faced a monster that, if he had lived, would surely kill again. Not kill pros like you and me, but unprotected innocents who were in the wrong place at the wrong time.

"And with Gushkov, I had a chance to kill him previously—a legitimate chance, because he was shooting at me. I found an excuse not to do it and it cost an innocent life. My guilt about that life probably pushed me into trying to atone by making Gushkov's death as unpleasant as possible. I own that—there's no excuse for it."

"Ben, I think I understand your actions better than my own. I executed that bastard on the spot. You can make up excuses for me, and I appreciate it, but I think I would have killed him whether or not he moved for a gun."

"But you don't know for sure?"

"No."

"Leave it at that. You'll never know for sure, so give yourself the benefit of a doubt. And if you hadn't fired, I would have, so the results would the same either way."

"But," I added, "be careful that you don't let your doubts screw you up on the next stand-off." She looked puzzled.

"Next time, with Whimple on your mind, you might hesitate too long, with ugly results. In a gunfight, go with your instincts—don't over-think the problem."

She laughed, then sobered.

"The soldier's solution. If it moves and shoots at you, shoot it. If it doesn't move and doesn't shoot at you, but it's wearing the wrong uniform, shoot it. Sorry, I shouldn't laugh. I know it's not that simple. But they don't give the bad guys special uniforms in my world."

"No, they don't, so you have to judge them by their actions and act accordingly. And you have to do it in an instant, and in accordance with a whole book of laws. I don't envy you law types one bit."

We stopped talking and fixed ourselves a nightcap apiece. We sat silently on the sofa, arms about each other's shoulders, and ruminated on the previous conversation. She eventually withdrew her arm and turned to me; I waited for more soul-searching.

"Ben, in our human behavioral courses, they tell us that after an emotional experience involving death, there is often an urge to procreate. Just nature trying to balance things out, perhaps."

"Yes," I said, "I think I've heard about that. Are you ready for bed yet?" She was.

CHAPTER 62

Logistics

The furor over the shooting of the serial killer had finally settled down, and the newspapers had tired of showing photos of a large bloody spot beside a fat-tired Super Cub. State and city police were still on a long-term search for buried bodies, guided by the pin-pricks in Charley Whimple's flight charts, and were still finding them. The Medical Examiner, Doc Rogers, was overwhelmed with old corpses needing identification, and next of kin nation-wide were being shocked into deep grief by notifications of his findings.

Liz and I finally faced up to the probability of another parting. It was a beautiful Indian Summer day in mid-September, and we sat out on the patio by the bluff watching the sun prepare for its dive into a golden bank of clouds to the northwest.

"Ben, I have to either pull the pin or go back to work."

"I know."

"When I get back to Quantico, I'll probably be ordered out to my next station pretty quickly. After a bunch of psychological testing to determine if the shooting screwed up my mind, of course."

"You could play crazy, get a disability pension, and come live with me," I suggested. "I'm willing to swear you're nuts."

She ignored the comment.

"We've experienced a year apart," she said. "I don't know about you, but it was really hell for me until the initial shock dulled. Then I had the classes and my studies to divert my mind. It must have been worse for you."

As a typical male who never wants to show his softer side, I tried to respond honestly without sounding too pitiful.

"Liz, going anywhere we used to go, seeing the things we used to see together... It was painful. I shoved you out of my thoughts dozens of times every day. I'd imagine I got a flash of you in a crowd and crane my neck looking. I'd notice an attractive lady and get a stab of guilt for noticing. I'd be up on a mountain and remember the cautions you used to ram down my throat—sometimes do a stupid thing just to say, 'Liz isn't here now, you can do what you want.'

"And that's the manly version. I won't bore you with the sentimental version; I don't want you to see me cry."

"Must be hell to be a man and not be allowed to get sentimental," she said, a touch of irony in her voice.

"Well, we got by for a year," I said, "but how many more years do we want to waste? Do we ever want to marry? Do we ever want children? Time's getting short and our choices will narrow soon enough."

"The answer's pretty simple, Ben. I want to marry you. I want to have your children. And I want to be the first FBI woman ever to be Special-Agent-in-Charge of a station. All we have to do is figure out how to do all that while I'm still young enough to have the children."

We didn't discuss the subject further that evening, just sat together and watched the sun go down over our Alaska.

On the day Liz closed out the FBI report and finished her temporary duties in Alaska, she came home early. I was expecting her to pack up in readiness to fly out in the morning, and was already downhearted at the prospect.

"Ben," she said, "as of Monday morning I'm starting on ten days' leave. I'm yours and you're mine for two weeks." I started to open my mouth and she kissed it shut.

"Just listen. I get 30 days a year of annual leave. I could take it five days at a time, do the travelling on weekends, and be with you six times a year. It'll be expensive, and there'll be times it doesn't work out when I'm on a case somewhere. But maybe you'll need to travel to the lower 48 for some reason during the year; that could add to our together time."

I was blindsided by the idea—it was obviously too simple to work. There must be a catch somewhere.

"And just think," she continued, "with a couple of months of anticipation between visits—well, remember the night I came in out of the storm?"

I sat down at the kitchen table, determined to find something wrong with the scheme. Liz patiently waited, then fetched a couple of glasses and poured some of the good scotch.

"Do you think it'll really work?" I asked.

"Why don't we try? Or would you like to go back on the once-a-year schedule and stay pissed off at the world for 11 months?"

"Liz, if it works out without too much grief, we could think about marrying; many an Army marriage has held together under separations as bad as this one would be. And if you did happen to get knocked up somehow..."

"Whoa, Buster. Don't get carried away. I see this as a trial—I'm not ready for a leap into a whole new lifestyle yet. Hell, I might decide you're not my type after all. But let's do it!"

The ten days passed without incident, which was the way we preferred. We made another round of visits to our friends in Seward and Cooper landing, where Liz spent an afternoon giving informal combat pistol lessons to the Fuller Shop crowd. The rookie cop from Soldatna was in attendance, and paid strict attention.

We drove to Eureka for lunch at the Lodge, enjoying a round trip made golden by turning birch and aspen leaves. We laughed at corny jokes and bad puns, and teased and flirted with each other without thoughts of wrecked airplanes or serial killers shadowing the background.

We were almost anxious to try our staged separation, knowing that the pain of this parting couldn't possibly be as excruciating as the one a year past. When I took her to the airport on the last day, I was too cowardly to see her to the gate. We had said our good-byes the night before, the way we had done a year ago, but with optimism and fewer tears.

I got home just in time to watch her plane lift from the airport over Knik Arm, circle around to the north east, and disappear over the mountains toward Seattle.

THE END

AUTHOR'S NOTES

The Airplane

The C-47 we know as the Red Starred Lady would have been one of 10,174 built during WW2. They were officially named Skytrain by the manufacturers, but were called Dakotas by the Canadians and British. This may have been due to the nomenclature, Douglas Aircraft Company Transport Aircraft.

705 were transferred to Russian ownership and used on the ALSIB (Alaska-Siberia) Lend-Lease shuttle.

According to records, 133 planes of all types crashed in Canada and Alaska during the Lend-Lease operation.

C-47 aircraft were the workhorses of the Allies during the war. They flew critical cargo to fighting forces on all fronts and back-hauled our soldiers, dead, wounded, or living, home from the war. They dropped our paratroopers over Normandy, and towed troop-carrying gliders into Holland. During the Cold War, they served humanity during the Berlin Air Lift.

C-47's have been fitted with skis, floats, and cannon, their rugged durability and versatility adapting them to many experimental or innovative uses.

After the war, surplus C-47's were used by hundreds of start-up airlines in every corner of the globe, and are still serving in many out-of-the-way locales.

Other Russian Losses

Other Russian-crewed aircraft went down under conditions similar to those which proved fatal to the Red Starred Lady. In the National Military Cemetery at Fort Richardson, Alaska, are the graves of eleven WW2 Russian military personnel who perished during the Lend-Lease airlift. Their headstones are identical to those of the American dead among whom they lie, and their names are inscribed on the stones.

WW2 Lend-Lease

The WW2 Lend-Lease program is adequately described in the body of this novel. The exploitation of the program for espionage and political purposes by Russia is recounted in detail in Major George Racey Jordan's book, "From Major Jordan's Diaries", now out of print and difficult to find.

Aside from the establishment of a corps of "sleeper" agents within the United States, the Russians are estimated to have built their first atomic bomb years sooner than expected because of the technology and the uranium compounds smuggled via the ALSIB Route.

Women in the FBI

In my haste to find a suitable partner for Ben, I have somewhat distorted the time line during which women found a place as agents of the FBI. In "Washtub Gold", I had them meet during a murder investigation in 1967. Actually, the first women were admitted immediately after J. Edgar Hoover's death in 1972. (Yes, there was a connection.) The science of "profiling" began to be studied during the same year, so Liz was at the right place at the right time.

Liz aspires to be the first woman Special Agent in Charge of an FBI Field Office. The first woman agent actually holding the job of SAIC was "Birdie" Pasenelli, who took over the Field Office in Anchorage, Alaska, in 1992.

Profiling

The case of serial killer Charley Whimple was shamelessly spun off the famous Robert Hansen case. Hansen, a baker by trade, kidnapped, tortured, raped, or murdered more than two dozen women over many years. He was eventually caught and jailed, largely with the aid of FBI profiling experts. Agent Elise Nichole found a more permanent solution.

ACKNOWLEDGMENTS

My deep appreciation and belated thanks to my friend and sometime consultant, the late Dr. Don Rogers. Don's advice and experience were invaluable assets during the writing of this book. I deeply regret that he is not here to enjoy it.

My thanks to my "test readers", Nancy, Marge, and Kara, and my daughters Deborah and Cheryl. Again, I cling to the ladies for support and advice—they are gentler in their criticism.

And, as always, Debi Gordon of First Edition Design Publishing, who always knows where to land that swift kick when my natural inertia sets in.

Printed in Dunstable, United Kingdom

74515984R00139